Chapel Veils, Cough Drops and Queen for a Day: Being a Kid in the 1950s

By Barbara Lockard

Cover Design by Rhonda Hile

Copyright © 2020 Barbara Lockard
All rights reserved
ISBN: 9798564936309

Table of Contents

Growing Up – Cincinnati 1950s 1
Keeping Kids Busy Easy-Peasy 3
Two Kids, a Hill and a Huffy 7
Culture, Creepies and Corn Dogs, All in One Place 11
"…and She's Having Fun, Fun, Fun, ... 15
Chlorine, Yellow Ducks and Prohibition 21
Big Kids vs. Little Kids: A Good Time Was Had by All 25
Empty Wallets, Broken Bones and More Fun with Horses 29
Wigs, Hamburgers, Shoes and Unrealized Dreams 33
Shopping, Sin and the #21 Bus 37
Limburger Cheese, The Shooting Star and an Ethical Dilemma .. 41
Trick or Treat. Smell My Feet. 47
Purgatory, Disinfectant and Communists 51
We Don't Need No Education. . . in Saddle Shoes 55
A Paper Bag, Black Lace and a PBJ: 59
Memories (and Maybe Cures) Are Made of This 63
The Silver Lining May Just be Yellow Stamps 67
Why I'm Bat Shit Crazy. . . And so Are You (Probably) 71
Thoughts and General Comments on the Present-Day Insanity ... 75
Why It Sucks to be Old During a Pandemic 77
Sticks and Stones. . . and Pumpkins? 81
Why Do Old People Know This Stuff? 85
In the Name of Shopping 89
There's a Difference Between "Karen" and Kvetching! 93
Memories of Hoarding and Gouging 99

Oh, to be in East Jesus! 103
The Pandemic and the Black (Lab) Plague 105
Backyard Pools, Whirly-Thingys and Bullfinches 109
Five Things I'd Like to See in the Internet of Things 113
Products of the Past Should STAY in the Past 117

Growing Up – Cincinnati, 1950s

Keeping Kids Busy Easy-Peasy (if you don't mind a little danger)

So what if was unsanitary, unsafe and unhealthy, it was FUN!

Don't get me wrong. I feel for our kids in the midst of this COVID shutdown. Our neighbor's 10-year-old son kicks a soccer ball around listlessly. Girl Scouts meet on Zoom, and how can you socially distance in a swimming pool? (Everyone knows that kids' water recreation consists of close-contact Marco Polo!)

As summer looms with no organized activities to keep our youngsters entertained, I thought I'd share a few activities that helped my generation pass the hours on weekends and school breaks. Few of us had the funds to attend "sleep away" camp and aside from an occasional baton-twirling clinic, lessons and workshops were non-existent. We were left to rely on imagination, a ruthless sense of competition and a near-psychotic desire to cause ourselves great bodily harm. With the help of parents who had too many kids and too little time to worry about anyone over the age of 2, we enjoyed some unique amusements.

Collecting Pop Bottles

First, let's get our definitions straight. Where I grew up, "pop" was any carbonated beverage that came in a glass bottle. Flavors were cola, root beer and Lime Ricky. "Soda" was served in a tall glass with ice cream and a skinny spoon. Flavors were chocolate and chocolate. I didn't realize that moving 160 miles away would force me to turn to Rosetta Stone to learn the native language. Here, one refers to cans of Diet Coke and Mountain Dew as "soda." How uppity can you get?

Collecting pop bottles was a rite of passage in the 1950s. Merchants charged a 2-cent deposit on each glass bottle and paid that same 2-cents for each bottle returned. Since most adults couldn't be bothered with returning bottles for a mere pittance, discards were fair game for kids and parents never questioned where funds earned were spent. Older siblings usually claimed the cash, enlisting younger brothers and sisters to shimmy into sewers or under abandoned houses to retrieve an empty Barq's Grape or Choc-ola receptacle. If you survived, you maybe got a couple of pennies for your trouble.

Return on investment was huge in the bottle collecting business. The only equipment needed was a rusted-out wagon to transport the bottles. Territories were staked out and defended. Our favorite spot was the covered area behind the Pure Oil Station. Because of the shelter it provided it was frequented by what my mother called, "derelicts." This group of wandering gentlemen often spent a night or two at Chez' Pure Oil, sucking down some pop and probably listening to classical music before retiring for the night. We kids reaped the rewards in the daylight hours, scooping up empty, sticky containers of Coke, cream soda and Orange Crush. This was not a hygienic activity. Sometimes there was pop left in the bottle which we dumped, usually on our sneakers. Once I found a bottle with a dead mouse stuck in the neck. The little guy had, apparently, underestimated his size in a quest for a sugar-laden sip and found himself trapped. We actually tried to get a little more money for the bottle with the mouse, but the owner of R&H Delicatessen wasn't buying it. (A measly 2-cents for this freak of nature?)

Play in the Lightning

This is the God's-honest truth. Whenever thunder sounded in the distance, my mother would command my sister and I to don our swimsuits and get ready to play in the deluge. She didn't believe that lightning was a threat. She didn't know anyone who had been struck by lightning and thought its danger was totally overrated. So we'd cram into our last year's suits and jump around ecstatically in the downpour. A favorite variation was lying in the gutter where the water rushed to reach the nearest sewer grate. The warm, dirty water washing over you while lightning struck a tree 5 feet away was something like a kid's Nirvana.

Defying all odds, we survived years of playing in Level 5 thunderstorms. My only injury occurred when I decided to lie, face up, in a large puddle in front of our house. True to form, my sister yelled at me to move because she wanted to ride her bike through the puddle. I refused. Without warning, she proceeded to pedal hard, running over my abdomen without looking back. Miraculously, I sustained no major organ damage, although I do still bear the tread marks of a Schwinn across my gut. I also bear a grudging respect for my sister who proved that she's no woman to be messed with.

Yo-yo Tournaments, or, "Around the World" Can Lead to Head Injuries

The kids in my neighborhood were keenly competitive. One whiff of a possible contest or "tournament" had them salivating and honing their skills in whatever was the trend of the day…Four-square, Hula Hoops, Monopoly or yachting. For about two summers, I recall that the Duncan yo-yo dominated our waking hours and yo-yo tournaments were held whenever two or more kids got together. Since a yo-yo was 49-cents (except for the rhinestone-studded Duncan Elite which was a dollar), just about everyone had a small collection. We practiced walk-the-dog, rock-the-baby, and swinging our Duncan's in a wide arc, a move called, "Around the World," which usually resulted in an audience member taking one on the head.

Once each summer, "Yo-yo Man," would visit the local mall, showing off an amazing set of tricks and inspiring all of us to work harder at our craft. I decided that I had an innate yo-yo talent and would pursue a scholarship to the Duncan Yo-yo Academy, forgoing any traditional career for the life of a traveling yo-yo savant. Maybe this is where I went wrong. I see it clearly now. I was never meant to be a marketing director/PR coordinator. God intended me to be Yo-yo Woman. Definitely a missed opportunity!

Just this week, I bought my 8-year-old granddaughter a six-pack of Duncan yo-yo's. The intent was to encourage her and her friends to learn the value of practice-makes-perfect and spend many happy hours together in friendly competition. She eagerly unwrapped a transparent red yo-yo and let it roll down the string. When it laid dead at her feet, she said, "It's broken," and grabbed a blue one. The blue one was "broken," too so she systematically worked her way through all six. "You should send these back," she insisted. "None of them work." (Somehow my life lesson got warped).

There are so many more enriching, exciting activities I could share, like doing stupid things on your bike, learning to dive in a 36-inch pool and knife games. This calls for a two-parter. Next week: If you think coronavirus is scary, try this!

Two Kids, a Hill and a Huffy

1950s Bike Riding not for the Faint of Heart!

Got caught up in the excitement last week while sharing some 1950s outdoor activities with today's quarantined youth. True to my word, I present Part 2 in this post; more "How-did-we-ever-live-through-this?" ways we enjoyed the long days of summer, totally uninhibited and always unsupervised.

Some Called it Bicycling

Our two-wheelers were such a big part of life that biking deserves its own treatise. From my sister, who, on a dare, rode her Schwinn down the steep concrete steps of Westwood School, to our paperboy, who could ride no-handed while rolling a Cincinnati Post and tossing it with pinpoint accuracy to a subscriber's porch, we were all centaurs. Half bike, half unwashed kid, we spent the summer astride our Huffys, Raleighs, and Roadmasters. Well…astride MOST of the time.

My parents liked to party. Some weekends, they'd go off for a day lasting long into the evening, leaving my sister and me to survive by our wits and bravado. I remember one such July Saturday when we decided to tackle the ultimate biking challenge. The name still conjures up pictures of missing teeth and "minor" head injuries. White Street.

Our hometown was known as the City of Seven Hills, and I think all seven were within five miles of my house. White Street was a hill running off of a hill that headed downtown. Similar in reputation to Lombard Street in San Francisco (except it was steeper and without curves) White Street beckoned to every daredevil underage cyclist with promises of grandeur and maybe a broken bone or two. People actually fell off of White Street. No, I don't mean fell <u>down</u> on White Street, I mean they literally fell <u>off</u>

of the sidewalk landing in an infinite roll until hitting Queen City Avenue at the bottom.

It didn't matter that my sister and I were ages 10 and 6 respectively. It didn't matter that we lived 3 miles down a main thoroughfare from our destination. It didn't matter that we had no 10-speeds or even 3-speeds at the time. We rode. She on her expensive, bourgeois Schwinn and me on a hand-me-down, 20-inch Huffy. To make it more picturesque, a thunderstorm was brewing when we reached the top of the Bermuda Triangle of hills. I froze. I could not keep my Buster Brown sandals from stomping backward on the pedals, setting the brakes and feeling hot tears forming in my eyes. My older sibling was never at a loss for comforting words. "Chicken!" she yelled. "Well, wait here for me, you big baby!"

She was usually a quiet and reasonable young lady, but there was something about a bike that brought out the Vin Diesel in her. She pushed off, disappearing at breakneck speed while I sat at the top of the hill, knowing I would return home sisterless (if I could remember the way home.) Then, miraculously, she reappeared toward the bottom of that hill, skidding to a stop and raising clasped hands in a victory salute to herself. It must have been the adrenalin rush that enabled her to ride back up. Either adrenalin or quads conditioned by 10 years of hill work. Since she wasn't speaking to me, we rode home in silence. I remain embarrassed. White Street is still on my bucket list. I think I could make it down. Riding back up would require a heart transplant, portable oxygen and nitroglycerin.

As I recall, my parents arrived home around 9 that evening, happy in the way that only 15 martinis could make you and bearing gifts of cocktail peanuts and frilly toothpicks. When asked how we had spent our 12 hours alone, my sister responded, "You can't go anywhere with HER!" Case closed. The secret was never revealed…until now.

The only bike adventure more daring than the White Street incident also involved my sister and, believe it, a tricycle! You see, people were known to stretch the law a bit in the 50s. For instance, parents could send a very minor child to the store with a note instructing the shopkeeper to send Myrna home with a bottle of Four Roses, two Red Hot Smokies and a racing form, and "make sure to give her the right change!" It was a common practice.

My sister had inherited a big maroon tricycle from someone on my father's side of the family. One summer day, my mother found herself stuck at home with a toddler (me) and fresh out of cigarettes. There was only one answer. She hastily scribbled, "Please send a pack of Lucky Strikes and the right change" on a piece of looseleaf paper and stuffed it and a dollar into my five-year-old sibling's pocket. Vin Diesel was off, to Welch's Delicatessen, one mile away and on the other side of Dead Man's Curve. My sister confessed just today that not only did she return with cigs, but spent the change on a grape ice cream cone which she ate on the return trip. Not bad for someone who didn't have all of her baby teeth yet!

I started this post, truly believing that today's youth are too pampered and overprotected to even attempt the feats we relished as kids. As I wrap up, though, I see my neighbors' grandchildren though my front window. They are riding, helmetless on skateboards, screaming and beating each other with pool noodles. Maybe there's hope for us yet!

Culture, Creepies and Corn Dogs, All in One Place

1950s drive-in theaters were close to a kid's paradise!

There were no sweeter words on a hot 1950s summer night than my dad saying, "I think I'm in the mood for a movie." Keep in mind, the word "movie" here conjured up a lot more for a little kid than just sitting in front of a screen. It meant "drive-in movie," an experience that included danger (playground), adventure (finding your way to the bathroom), espionage (stealing your sibling's snack, blanket, etc.) and search and rescue (when you inevitably got lost winding your way from the restroom back to the car.)

We had three drive-in's in our west side Cincinnati area. There was the Auto-In, located conveniently near our home and adjacent to the Crookshank Rd. incinerator and landfill (known collectively as "the dump".) The Dent Drive-In, named for its location in Dent, Ohio and not for the condition of the cars after they left the premises, involved a short ride into the country. The Dent had a reasonable admission fee and car speakers that worked most of the time. The premier west side drive-in was the Ferguson Hills, newer and larger than the others, with more selections in its snack bar. The "Ferguson" also stayed open if it rained, providing determined customers with a device that fit over the top of their windshields and deflected even a heavy downpour.

There were other establishments, of course, but most located in remote areas, including the "east side" which was like crossing from South to North Korea as far as us west siders were concerned. The Twin Drive-in, in Reading, Ohio, had TWO screens and a capacity of about 10,000 cars. In high school, we would venture out to the Twin to catch horror fests of five or six movies. (Doctor on premises for those who faint from fright! Free doughnuts to those who survive until 4 a.m.!) I earned a free doughnut back in 1966, staying coherent through "The Bloody Butchers,"

"The Bloody Butchers 2," "Bloody Butchers Reunited," "Bloody Butchers, Next Generation" and "Bloody Butchers, Inc." (the animated version.)

Unlike my brave, swarthy high school self, as a kid I was terrified of movie monsters, but somehow drawn to the movies that made them famous. I begged my dad to take us to "I Was a Teenage Werewolf," but never saw the transition where Michael Landon became a horrifying creature just by basking in the light of the full moon. As soon as the creepy music would start, I'd duck behind the driver's seat and close my eyes just for good measure. This scenario was the same with "Frankenstein," "The Fly" and anything with Vincent Price. To this day, I don't think I've seen Landon in his full wolf regalia.

We didn't just see horror movies, though. The 50s drive-in was the poor man's exposure to great films like "On the Waterfront," "The Ten Commandments," "Witness for the Prosecution," and, yes, "The Blob" and "Seven Year Itch". My parents would elect to see something like "Oklahoma," an endlessly long musical, and we kids would go along and watch without a whimper. (We would have watched "50 Shades of Grey" if it meant a visit to the playground and scoring a Bit O' Honey from the snack bar). Note that parents made the decision on what movies to see during the 1950s and didn't bother to poll their kids to check if there was interest. If it was four hours long with subtitles, tough toenails to kids who couldn't yet read. Watch the movie or fall asleep.

Movies started at dusk. In pre-daylight savings time Ohio, that meant around 9 p.m. The theaters' playgrounds opened around 6. Enterprising mothers would make sure kids had adequate time on the cement and cast-iron play equipment, so they would sit quietly through a double feature if necessary. Mothers also came prepared with snacks for their broods. Snack bar food was expensive. I loved the cheeseburgers in their foil packets, but only tasted one or two in my drive-In career. My mom's snack of choice was a bag of grapes. . . healthy and less sugar than a frozen Snicker's, but not very sustaining for a 3+ hour film. "But, Mom, the Schmidt's get to pick what they want from the snack bar," I would whine. "Well, Doris Schmidt inherited her family's soup company, so she's got all kinds of money. When I inherit a soup company, you can have a cheeseburger," she'd retort.

"A big buttered popcorn and an extra-large Coke, a few chili dogs and man, I'm goin' broke, at the drive-in."

At the Drive-In
The Beach Boys

Inevitably, about halfway through the first feature, nature would call, which meant a trip to the snack bar/restroom/projection room building located directly in the center of the drive-in empire. Parents, deeply involved in the plot, didn't feel obligated to escort you. At age 5 or 6, you were expected to navigate through lines of Chevys, Fords and Ramblers, find the restroom, do your "business," and return, safely, to your car. It NEVER happened. Finding the building was easy. Finding your car in a sea of look-alike 1950s automobiles in the dark was nearly impossible. After about 90 minutes, Dad would dispatch my older sister to go find me and she usually did. This was after I had knocked on 50 windows of patrons who were making out, sleeping, passed out on beers brought from home, or just watching the movie. I never heard of any kids being abducted from a drive-in, but probably a lot were left behind by tired parents who took an inaccurate head count before leaving.

I understand that with the event of COVID-19, the few drive-ins that are left are making a comeback. They are hosting graduation ceremonies, concerts, and showing old movies. I've even heard of one that delivers pizza to your car, thanks to 21st-century GPS and the microwave oven. (Imagine the gall of robbing kids of the experience of traveling alone to the snack bar and disturbing young couples in compromising positions on the trip back)! As for our west side drive-ins, they concluded that 30 acres of prime real estate could have more value than a high-end parking lot. They are now urology offices, strip malls, Check Into Cash establishments and even a Wal-Mart. Bet they don't even have playgrounds or offer free doughnuts. As for trying to sneak in a bag of grapes. . . forget it!

"...and She's Having Fun, Fun, Fun, 'Til Her Daddy took the Volkswagen Away!"

With apologies to the Beach Boys

My father had a difficult life, and as a result, not much made him angry or upset. He was, however, driven beyond human endurance trying to teach me to drive a stick shift at age 16 in the parking lot of Gamble Junior High School.

Dad was able to procure questionable vehicles which he referred to as "go to work" cars. True, they could also be called "death traps," but at 16 in the 1960s, ANY car was better than riding the bus. As we ground around the Gamble asphalt, I learned a Renault Dauphine with a devious clutch and a solitary gear shift as its only accessory, was not just ANY car.

"Let it out easy," yelled my father, as I popped the clutch and stalled the puke-green vehicle for the thousandth time. "This is a stupid car," I yelled back near tears. I would have unfastened my seatbelt and run home, except my enterprising dad had cut the seatbelts out of the Renault before presenting it to me. "You don't want to be stuck in this car in a wreck," he cautioned. "Better to fly out through the windshield."

After a few weeks, we gave up. After all, what kind of name is Renault Dauphine? It sounds like something Joan of Arc would have crusaded for. "And Joan charged into battle, carrying the flag of the Renault Dauphine; leader of France, defender of the faith, and great gas mileage."

Next, I was gifted with a 1960 Corvair. If the Renault was devoid of options, the Corvair was positively Spartan. It had seats and a gearshift. There was nothing on the dashboard and I honestly don't remember it having headlights. For those born after 1950, let me inform you that the Corvair came to fame as the topic of Ralph Nader's book, "Unsafe at Any Speed." Among other faults, the Corvair's exhaust manifold would sometimes leak, pumping carbon monoxide into the heater. This could cause drivers on long trips to pass out…at any speed.

I loved my Corvair. True to its simplistic style, it was white with a rear, air-cooled engine. I was attending a small, Catholic college in Northern Kentucky at the time, and agreed to take on some additional riders to pay for gas. With four of us sealed inside, I discovered that the Corvair had a top speed of 40 mph. Driving to higher education on I-75 was a challenge, but I was up to it. I would start gaining speed around the Western Hills Viaduct in preparation for my grand entrance onto America's busiest north/south corridor. Still in second gear, with the (air-cooled) engine screaming, I put it into third just as I merged into the right-hand lane that would take me across the Ohio border. If luck was with me, I wouldn't have to change lanes the entire trip. I never had the near-death experience of spraying straight CO out of my heater, but often thought of taking a canary along on my forays to school. Dead bird means turn off the heat and open the window!

The Corvair met its demise when my friend Patty put her foot through the floor as she was easing into the passenger seat one fine summer evening. It was followed by a succession of "go to work" cars, including the Chodge, a yellow station wagon that was half Chevy and half Dodge. I had semi-learned to drive a standard shift by then but was attending the University of Cincinnati in the Chodge years. For the uninitiated, Cincinnati is built on hills, and "UC" is located at the top of one of them.

Are You There, God? It's Me, Barb.

Every time I drove McMillan Street hill, I said the Stick Shift Novena. "Please God, I will do the nine First Fridays if you let me make the light at the top of the hill." (This plea was followed by three Our Father's and three Hail Mary's.) If God was benevolent, I would cruise, smiling through the light and continue on to hunt for a parking spot. In the case of a vengeful God, however, I would catch the red light and have to sync my clutch and gearshift just right to avoid rolling backwards into the driver behind me, or worse, rolling back to the bottom of the hill only to start the Novena all over again.

Although I did not graduate from college until age 36, I did graduate to newer and slightly more reliable vehicles. My first new car was an AMC Gremlin. There was a 1963 Pontiac Catalina; blue with one green fender, and I seem to remember a dark green station wagon that I eventually abandoned in one of my former employers' parking lots. All was well with the world, until, in 1977, I discovered the Volkswagen.

Old Volkswagens were insidious. They were like the Gremlins in the movie; cute and cuddly, but don't feed them after midnight and don't expect to drive anywhere in them unscathed.

Even though, at an MSRP of $6,500, the Volkswagen Rabbit was a bit rich for our blood, my ex-husband and I just had to have one. The metallic green box had front wheel drive, a snazzy leather interior and boasted 42 m.p.g. We drove it from the showroom, heady from the new car smell and chomping at the bit to take road trips that had previously been off limits due to "unreliable" vehicles. It was on a trip to Louisville, Kentucky, with the odometer reading 6,000 miles, that the entire braking system went kaput. The Rabbit literally would not stop without running into a solid object. It was the ironic nature of the Volkswagen that, while it would not stop at a red light, it did start coming to a stop in the high-speed lanes of interstates. I would be barreling along at 65 m.p.h., then notice that things had gotten incredibly quiet. Voila! The engine had died. I call this the first version of "cruise" control.

There are two code words among Volkswagen mechanics that they resort to when all else fails … "fuel injectors." "You'll have to replace the fuel injectors," said one German car expert after another. And so, after paying $250, only to come to a halt in the center lane of I-275 during Friday rush hour…or while flying down the Ronnie Ray-gun Highway, I'd consult yet another expert and learn, "You'll have to replace the fuel injectors." After a year, we traded the Rabbit for a nice American car; not as glamorous, but no code words.

A Vintage Deception

I should have sworn off Volkswagens, and almost did, until, in 2004, my daughter brought home a flyer being circulated at her high school. "For Sale," it read, "Vintage 1981 VW Cabriolet convertible, completely restored, leather seats, runs fine, $3,500 firm." Sarah and I agreed that the car was the epitome of cute. It had even won the "Coolest Car" designation in the high school yearbook. I think I wanted it more than she did. The sellers attested that they had never experienced much engine trouble and the car had taken their son to school and back every day for two years. We christened it, "the Putt-Putt." I wrote a check. Dumb, dumb, dumb!

The little car's first sign of distress came the day after purchase when my husband and I were driving around the neighborhood. Like a ghost from 1977, the engine just stopped, stranding us a few blocks from home. After "resting," it started a few hours later. Driving her friends to school, my daughter discovered that the heater didn't work and took to carrying Goodwill winter coats for her freezing passengers. Periodically, the "oxygen" light would glow on the wood-grain dashboard, prompting the carpool to fall on the floor, hands around their throats, gasping, "Oxygen, oxygen!" Desperate, I took it to an automotive electrical specialist and didn't hear from him for three weeks. "Where's my car?" I finally got up the courage to ask. "I have it locked up," he replied. "I'm really mad at it, so I thought it would be better for us not to see each other for a while."

I should have known the Putt-Putt was plotting something sinister when Sarah decided to drive it 40 miles to the Toledo Zoo. She returned late that evening, dragging a belt underneath and dripping gasoline. It seems that nearly all of the gas had leaked out on the trip and she had to keep stopping to fill up. We decided it was time to call in the ultimate expert . . .a mechanic in a small town near us who was known throughout the State for his prowess with European cars. We waited five weeks for an appointment. I felt a great relief, dropping my sickly baby off to this man. I knew he would make things right…the stalling, the random lights, the broken belts and the lack of heat. I called the next day for the verdict.

"It took me a while, but I know what's wrong. It'll be pretty expensive, but I think it will solve your problems. You need to replace the fuel injectors."

Chlorine, Yellow Ducks and Prohibition

Swimming in the 50s was my first mind-blowing, chemical experience!

In the 1950s our swim season usually started in mid-June. With no heated pools, a late May start in Cincinnati's fickle weather could mean snowflakes on your "nose and eyelashes" while doing the backstroke. A heated pool was one that had basked in the 90-degree, 99 percent humidity of July and August until it was the temperature of bathwater and the consistency of cooking oil.

My favorite swimming hole (and it was pretty much a hole) was The Commons. Our neighborhood city park, The Commons was 50 acres of dusty grass, tennis courts, ball fields and, blissfully, a pool. At 3-and-a half-feet deep with murky gray water, the pool drew hundreds of kids daily each summer. My sister reminds me that the pool was drained every evening and re-filled in the early morning hours. Filters had not yet been invented.

Still, the customers and staff stretched this questionable body of water to its limits. Kids learned to dive in that pool, God love 'em, risking traumatic brain injury perfecting their two-and-a-half with a tuck into water that barely reached their waists. "Competitive" swimming consisted of staying one step ahead of Big Daniel, who would grab an unsuspecting swimmer by the shoulders and proceed to sit on their head. (Looking back, it strikes me as odd that a 27-year-old male would hang out in a pool full of kids. Better we didn't know.)

The Commons was also my first experience in flaunting child labor laws. At precisely 10 a.m. and 3 p.m. every day, a whistle would blow, signaling all swimmers to take their positions poolside with feet extended into the cloudy abyss. Lifeguards would walk around dumping the contents of large plastic buckets into the pool. One could only guess at the chemical composition of the contents, most probably chlorine, battery acid and Windex. Then, another whistle and we'd all kick furiously, churning the white substance into the gray water. When the lifeguards were feeling particularly frisky, they'd allow us to get into the pool and start a "whirlpool," circling madly, then quickly reversing course, giggling as we fought against a current of our own creation. By summer's end, we all had white swimsuits and white feet up to the ankles.

Oh, the Coveted Duck!

We future Olympians, however, began to crave more than just the dead man's float with wildly flailing arms. We'd heard from our country club friends that there were such things as strokes that could get you across the pool faster, while looking cool and effortless; strokes like freestyle, breaststroke and, the ultimate skill, the flip turn. We begged our moms for swim lessons, which meant a $5 charge for the series and a weekly trip to an indoor pool at Western Hills High School. The pool was tiled and freezing. Indoor pools were, also, not heated and did not have the access to hot sun and steamy outdoor temperatures.

To appreciate our swimming goals, one has to understand the intricacies of the Duck System. Participants were issued a plastic patch with a colored duck for each swim test they successfully completed. A red "beginner" duck meant you could, basically, stand in the pool for five minutes without drowning. The blue "intermediate" duck showed the world that you could swim the length of the pool with no lifeguard intervention. It was the yellow "swimmer" duck that we all aspired to. I dreamed of returning to The Commons, a yellow duck proudly displayed on the leg opening of my now white swimsuit.

I never earned that duck. To this day, even though I have completed a shaky triathlon, I cannot glide effortlessly through the water. Swimming has always been a major effort for me, although I once worked my way up to 20 struggling laps. (An adult swim instructor once yelled at me, "Barb, with all of that effort, GO SOMEWHERE!") At age 8, I learned that I would never be a Darla. Darla was tan and muscular with straight, blonde hair that managed to survive the onslaught of pool chemicals...plus, she wore the Yellow Duck. I was skinny and pale with red eyes and hair that felt like damp cotton. You were wrong, Sister Angeline, you can't be anything you set your mind to. You can't be old money, a ballet phenom, or Darla. Some of us must be satisfied with our lot in life.

Venturing Afar in the Swimming Pool World

Having mastered a clumsy freestyle (stroke, breathe, gulp, cough, stroke, breathe, gulp cough), we went in search of greener pastures...er, bluer waters. The 1950s and 60s was the era of the "for-profit" pool. People actually thought they could make a tidy sum collecting pocket change from us street urchins and maybe selling parents a soggy hot dog and a Coke. These are the ones I remember:

Gehrum's – (this isn't even on Google) Located on an estate off of Queen City Avenue, the urban legend was that the pool was built to fill in a liquor storage vault erected during Prohibition. Cost of entry was 35-cents. My mother complained because she had to drive us there and sometimes forgot to pick us up...no pay phone, no pool manager, just my sister and me and ghosts of bootleggers.

Harvest Home – Affectionately known as Pee Water Valley, Harvest Home pool was Cheviot, Ohio's cheapest form of childhood entertainment. Price of admission was 5-cents and they sold pretzel sticks for a penny. The pool had no diving board, ladder, steps or filter, but it was one step above The Commons, so always a treat.

Phillip's – Family-owned, Phillip's was the Taj Mahal of westside pools. Huge and surrounded by balconies, Phillip's was our favorite swimming destination when we could muster up the 50-cent admission charge. This pool was also home of the dreaded French Chew, a taffy candy bar that inflicted thousands of dollars of dental damage over the years. Oh yes, Phillip's is still in operation and now boasts 80 umbrella tables and serves cappuccino...cappu-wha'? Just give us a Barq's, man!

Meadowbrook – Located outside the city limits, Meadowbrook was fed by "sparkling artesian well water." Even on a sweltering August day, water temperature was about 45-degrees. After a day's swimming at Meadowbrook, you had to sit in front of a space heater for a few hours to thaw out. We knew when our friends went to Meadowbrook because of their blue lips and frosty eyebrows.

As far as I know, none of our gang ever became a threat to Mark Spitz, but swimming in the summer was an experience that rivaled Christmas morning. To this day, when I smell chlorine, I get goosebumps in anticipation of a water slide and penny pretzel. As I watch my granddaughter execute a perfect backstroke across her heated swim club pool, I'm sort of sorry she'll never get to enjoy making a whirlpool in a vat of pool chemicals or bragging about surviving a few hours at Pee Water Valley.

Big Kids vs. Little Kids: A Good Time Was Had by All

In our schoolyard, playing outside of your weight class was encouraged!

You can tell a lot about a generation by the games they play(ed). Today's kids are obsessed with Call of Duty and Madden NFL, games that provide the thrill of soldiering or football without actually having to leave your chair. Worst injury could be a strained thumb or high cholesterol. Regardless of your stand on video games, you have to admit that it makes sense to be comfortable and safe during recreational activities.

Now, MY generation chose instead to play its games on cement; games that pitted 250 lb. kids against 45 lb. kids and usually involved knocking someone down or throwing someone across the playground. Call of Duty? Child's play compared to wearing just Keds and pedal pushers into battle against an opponent twice your age and weight!

Our elementary schoolyard was divided into sections during recess for different age groups. To be honest, we did not honor these boundaries and considered them an affront to our attempt at recreational diversity. (Actually, it was much more fun to see the carnage caused by small, immoveable forces interacting with very large, fast-moving objects). We would often join the entire school together in such mentally-stimulating activities as Red Rover, Swinging Statues, Freeze Tag and Jump Rope.

Red Rover – Invented by Vlad the Impaler in the 15th century, Red Rover involved a line of kids facing another line of kids, about 50 ft. apart. Although the "official" Red Rover rules state that kids must only join hands, in our world you could connect your line by grasping wrists, forearms, or holding a kid's flannel shirt sleeve in your teeth. Playing on grass was recommended, but blacktop was more thrilling and didn't leave grass stains on your school pants. . . only blood stains.

The object of the game was to have a player from one team break through the line of the other team. This was best accomplished by aiming for a weak link, or two kids with arms that resembled Creamettes. (Red Rover was the inspiration for "elbow" macaroni). One team would call out, "Red Rover, Red Rover, We call (insert name) over". Insert name would charge like a raging bull toward some poorly developed opponents. If he or she managed to break through, they could bring the kids on either side of the break back to their own team. This was assuming that someone hadn't called 9-1-1 because Red Rover was notorious for broken collar bones. If Jake Lamotta didn't manage to rupture the chain, he stayed on the other team. A winner was declared when one team had all the kids. Often a team would forfeit because of orthopedic injuries.

I particularly liked Red Rover because it had a true element of danger. We all knew kids who walked around most of the summer in a hard cast covering their upper body from shoulder blades to clavicle, thanks to "taking one for the team." There were whispered rumors of playmates who were trampled or hit so hard that they failed several grades and thought every day was Tuesday. Red Rover was my game of choice even though there were a few others nearly as thrilling.

Swinging Statues – Looking back on it, there really was no goal, indeed, no winners, in Swinging Statues. Another "big kid" vs. "little kid" game, the swinger was usually an overdeveloped sixth-grader, while the "swingee" was one of the second-grade tykes who still used a step-stool to wash his hands. The swinger would swing the little kid around like a hammer throw and, having built up adequate velocity, would release the tiny one who usually landed somewhere in the school yard (or just a little outside of its confines.) True to the game's name, the swingee would try to land in a pose reminiscent of an ancient Greek sculptor, or a 7-year-old Venus de Milo. While there were no winners, there were often losers. These were the kids who may have hit the exterior wall of St. Catharine's Church or landed in a dumpster on their way to artistic expression. Again, no goal, no winners, but lots of laughs!

Freeze Tag- Similar to Swinging Statues in redeeming social value, Freeze Tag turned the tables, allowing little kids to be "it," while the big kids ran around in erratic circles waiting to be tagged. Once tagged, the runner would have to . . . you guessed it. . . freeze! Oftentimes, a large runner was known to ignore the slight tap from a pint-sized "it," and continue to race around the yard with his small nemesis clinging to his belt and yelling, "I said freeze. FREEZE!"

Jump Rope – This activity was as varied as the source and type of materials used for the main playing piece. . . the rope. I want to emphasize that 1950s parents would have busted a gut if asked to "buy" a jump rope. Not for us, one of those Disney Princess, polyethylene ropes with handles that light up and play "Let it Go." No, our ropes were usually a piece of clothesline, hacked off by a harried Mom. If the rope was too long, you wrapped it around both wrists. Too short? Jump a little higher! In a pinch, ropes could also be recycled packing twine (dangerous), a couple of dog leashes clipped together, or a garden hose; heavy, but great for knocking out a jumper who was hogging the show.

Single jumping was OK, but a long rope with turners on both ends was de rigueur in our neighborhood. Of course, everyone wanted to jump and no one wanted to turn the rope. The first response to, "Hey, let's play jump rope," was always, "No ender! No ender!" Still, we were an altruistic group, realizing that selfless service benefitted the entire community. We devised our own logarithm for determining how long you could jump and how long you had to "turn." It's my belief that the reason our generation has undergone so many rotator cuff surgeries was early damage incurred by turning a rope through 125 iterations of "Spanish Lady."

Even our seemingly sedentary games sometimes caused injury or disability. Kids who spent entire summers playing Jacks on a concrete front porch, bore callouses on the outside of their hands where there was, formerly, intact skin. Dehydration and catatonia were the by-products of marathon Monopoly playing, and many a child had a finger impaled on a Pick-up-Stix. Face, it, we were adventure seekers with parents too preoccupied with feeding and clothing a family to obsess about our personal safety.

So, if our generation is to be defined by the games we played, let's say we are fearless, spontaneous, independent and not afraid to tackle something bigger than ourselves. Oh yes, most of us also have puzzling pleasant memories of how we got that scar, bump, twitch or limp. No pain, no gain!

Empty Wallets, Broken Bones and More Fun with Horses

Riding to hounds has no place in a blue-collar world!

Those damn horses messed me up. Suddenly obsessed at age 9 with galloping, rearing and jumping images of equine splendor, I collected statues and pictures until even my dad (who worked 20 hours a day) took notice. What my parents thought was a passing phase, however, was more than they ever suspected. I didn't just want to amble around on a pony, I wanted to ride hunters and jumpers. This west side Cincinnati kid, whose mom drove a dented 1954 Chevy, wanted to join the Camargo Hunt. She wanted straight blonde hair, an old-money name and braces. This child, whose grandparents still spoke "low" German at home, didn't understand why she couldn't be a debutante.

"William and Marie Wanstrath present to society, their granddaughter, Barbara "Buffy" Lockard, at the Hudepohl Distillery on Saturday, the nineteenth of October. Members of the Bachelors' Cotillion will serve as escorts, assuming they can clock out early from their shift at Lunkenheimer."

At age 10, I began serious riding lessons with a crazy woman my mother had met at the laundromat. (Most of the influential people in my life had their origins at Duds & Suds or The Soapbox.). Through a messy divorce, this riding instructor had laid claim to a 20-acre farm and taken to playing Chopin in her underwear in the barn. Of course, I had to work for part of my lesson fee, hurling bales of hay through a chute and cleaning endless stalls.

After a few years, I moved on to her "ex," a former Cavalry officer who ran his students through hill and dale on a bunch of retired racehorses…psychopaths, all of them! My mount of choice was a 17-hand chestnut named "Bimbo." I survived our woodland forays by wrapping his reins around my palms and wedging my hands into his neck. As long as he couldn't move his head or stretch his neck, I could control him. If he managed to snatch the reins from my hands, Bimbo and I could easily wind up in Kentucky! As we flew past him on the way to the Ohio border, the instructor would yell at my 72-pound frame, "Geez, Barb, control that horse would you!"

The Equine Money Pit

Like all parents bent on financial self-destruction, mine purchased a horse for their pre-debutante daughter and arranged monthly fees at a local boarding stable. (At that time, full care was $32. Today, it's more like $600!). My steed was a chunky white animal that I eventually trained so well I could guide his moves telepathically. Had he possessed the right confirmation and breeding; he would have brought top dollar in the local horse market. As it was, he was a "grade" horse, who earned his share of second-place ribbons at 4-H shows.

Somehow, we found each other; a group of kids, ages 8 to 25-years-old, who spent every day after school and 10 hours on weekends at "the barn." We rode, groomed, bathed, cleaned tack and breathed manure. There were fraternal twins who owned a stunning pinto named Apache; a future Playboy Bunny with "Rebound," a 17.2-hand, Roman-nosed thoroughbred who, true to her name, actually bounded about 30 feet every time she was asked to canter. There was a frail heart patient whose wealthy father had been horse-traded into buying her a 4-year-old unbroken filly; an engaged couple with a pony they thought would grow into a horse someday, and a redheaded 20-year-old who kept her second horse a secret from her parents. One young man showed up on a Saturday with a buckskin mare who gave birth that night to a buckskin foal. Since the young owner was unaware of his mare's pregnancy and now had to pay board on two horses, the first thing he uttered on seeing the new baby was, "Dammit!" And that became the foal's name. Little Dammit and his mother were the talk of the stable for weeks!

Don't Worry, You're Safe?

Eventually, my family moved to a small place on a rural road and my horse moved with us. I rode mostly on weekends, usually by myself, through the 1,600 acres of Cincinnati's Mt. Airy Forest. There were hills, ravines, wide and sometimes flooded creeks and fallen trees to jump over. I'd leave at 10 a.m. and sometimes not return until 6 p.m. My mother never worried. "Who's going to get you on a horse?" she'd ask. There was a transient home at the end of our street and the property made a convenient shortcut. I'd ride, oblivious, past groups of scruffy-looking men gathered around fire pits. Many were probably sexual predators, but, as my mother always said, "Who's going to get you on a horse?"

Riding also made you tough. I tried to get to know a new boarder one summer but concluded that she was a snob as she kept to herself and spoke very little to any of us barn rats. Imagine my surprise when I was informed that she had been trail riding a few weeks prior and fell forward off of her horse while traveling downhill. Her horse stepped on her face, breaking her jaw. Her mouth was literally wired shut for the summer. It's not that she was unfriendly, she couldn't talk and took all of her meals through a straw. Ironically, her father was an oral surgeon, which lead my mother to say, "Oh, she gets free medical care. Not so shabby!"

As an adolescent and adult, I continued to ride off and on for several years, before giving it up for things like having children and working full time while going to school. Then, about five years ago, a friend convinced me to pursue it again through the riding program of a local, private university. We went at it seriously, working on dressage and even cross-country jumping. I learned that horses needed a LOT more in 2015 than they did in 1960. Today, they need supplements, chiropractors, specialized farriers, blankets, sheets, vitamins, colic insurance, imported tack and leather-bound grooming tools. Each week was another couple of hundred dollars for schooling, trimming, saddle-fitting, fly spray and (yuck) worm medicine. I learned where the term "horse poor" came from. Like someone on oxycontin, I still kept at it. Riding a horse was the closest I could come to being that debutante. Riding a horse separated me from the masses and walking around in riding boots was a continual high.

And, then, about two years ago I simply gave it up. It was too expensive and for an almost 70-year-old, too dangerous. I would get a dog, I reasoned; a well-bred dog and train him in agility. So today, I have gone from being dragged around an indoor arena by an off-the-track-thoroughbred to being dragged around an agility course by an extremely "un-agile" 110-pound Labrador Retriever. It's a little cheaper and a little safer…but not much!

Wigs, Hamburgers, Shoes and Unrealized Dreams. They Were ALL There!

Our local mall was "paradise found" for kids.

In the 1950s, for after-dinner recreation, families often took a drive. This meant piling everyone into the Chevy or Oldsmobile and making a beeline for the country. Not only was it scenic, but with windows rolled down, the country air cooled the car interior by about 20 degrees. Car air conditioners hadn't been invented yet, and besides, it was more fun to stick your nose out the "no draft" and gulp in air that smelled like new mown hay. . . and fertilizer.

It was on one of those trips I heard my dad comment that a large company was building something called a "shopping center," on the very road on which we were driving. My 4-year-old mind couldn't quite grasp the idea. So, it was a bunch of stores joined together where you could park your car and actually walk from groceries, to hardware, to a place that served Kentucky Fried Chicken? Without crossing a street? What a concept! It was no rumor. In 1954, Western Hills Plaza (WHP) opened its many doors and became a location where I spent a good part of my youth learning the meaning of retail therapy.

From age 9 to about 12, my best friend and I would spend every Saturday practicing the following routine: Search couch cushions, blackmail your sister, or use any means possible to hustle up some cash. (This usually resulted in a grand total of about 60-cents); meet somewhere on Lischer Avenue; walk the mile or so to our shopping mecca and begin a day of total materialism. For two Catholic girls, this was probably just a little bit sinful and we should have been giving our hard-earned cash to missionaries or saving for a Pagan Baby. Not gonna' happen!

First, we'd hit Carter's, the only full-service restaurant in the mall. You could get a hamburger for 35-cents, but I never seemed to have enough to get "fries with that." With a combined expenditure of 70-cents, we'd sit in a booth and giggle for the better part of an hour, making the big spenders wait for our table. Kids like us were probably responsible for the demise of Carter's. If you happened to have stock in the restaurant chain and are now living in abject poverty, I salute you. You gave Patti and me some great times.

Dimes Add Up!

From Carter's, it was on to our favorite store, Woolworth's. Why was it that "five and dime" stores lost their popularity and, ultimately, their place in American culture? Woolworth's had everything . . . well, at least everything a 10-year-old kid could want. First off, it was cheap. Also, there were lots of options to spend your remaining 25-cents. You could choose from an assortment of toys, games, goldfish, household goods, scarves, and, for some reason, wigs.

Our favorite aisle was the one with purses and wallets. We'd claw through the displays for wallets with photo sleeves stuffed with poorly printed pictures of celebrities. Since most of this fine leatherware was created in other countries, the celebrities' names were hilariously misspelled. Ricky Nelson was "Rod Neely," and Debbie Reynolds was always "Forever Debbie." Free laughs and, of course, we never put the shelves back in order.

Over the years, F.W Woolworth's became the location for our weekly "shopping spree." We'd start in Aisle 1, humming something like "Ride of the Valkyries" as we raced up and down each aisle, usually bumping into serious shoppers. (Maybe we were also responsible for the demise of Woolworth's?) We'd do the entire store in about three minutes and move on to bigger and better things. As we moved into the 1960s, every shopping center began competing for anchor stores. These were large department stores that had realized in order to survive, they needed locations in the suburbs as well as the mother ship downtown. At Western Hills Plaza, these stores were McAlpin's and the venerable Mabley & Carew. My family couldn't afford to shop on the main floors of these emporiums. Instead, we rode escalators down to the poorly lit basements where bargains hung on crowded racks and the dressing rooms weren't carpeted.

Tell Me I'm Fashionable!

Adorning the walls of the main floor junior departments were portraits of blonde young women in round-necked sweaters and pearls, their names and high schools on neat placards underneath each picture. These were the "Fashion Boards." It's one of my best kept secrets that I aspired to be on a Fashion Board. (The closest I have come is holding a Knight's Inn V.I.P. Card).

Fashion Boards had official meetings, where, I suppose, they set the trends for neighborhoods surrounding their particular stores. I could just hear April Simmons from St. Ursula Academy arguing that the west side was indeed ready for madras. We weren't. There were maybe two preppies on the entire west side and they went to school on the east side. My older sister was considered "very cool" by her peers and she consistently wore tight gray flannel shorts and a white oxford shirt with her waist cinched by a red, 3" wide belt. Take that, fashionistas!

There were specialty stores, but we saved these for parent-accompanied visits. Our moms took us to Potter's Shoe Store before school started so we could get something with a "good fit." (There were actually people who spent their lives measuring and pressing down on kids' feet. Kinky!) There was a portrait studio and an appliance store that unabashedly used "bait and switch" as it's brand marketing. We patiently waited while our moms made a weekly deposit at one of the bank branches in the mall, sometimes starting a savings account there with the best of intentions. (I had $17 in my college fund in 1970; but then, classes at the University of Cincinnati were $12 per credit hour. I do not lie)!

As if toys, wigs and hamburgers weren't enough to satiate a 10-year-old on a fine September Saturday, WHP also had a small amusement park in its rear parking lot. I can still see the tiny ferris wheel that held an appeal for us long after we should have been too old. If we were still flush with 15-cents, we'd purchase a purple cotton candy there to eat on the walk home. In a day where there were no cell phones, tracking devices, or other means of knowing where your children were, we had been gone for more than 7 hours. . . but our parents never worried. My mom would greet me upon my return with the same mantra.

"How was the shopping center? I hope you didn't spend ALL your money!"

Shopping, Sin and the #21 Bus

This wasn't Amazon one-click. It was a true "experience!"

It was a Thursday morning in the 1950s and I was dressed in a shirtwaist dress, anklets, patent leather shoes and white gloves. No, we weren't on the way to church, a funeral or a coronation. My mom, sister and I were waiting for the #21 bus to take us shopping at Shillito's (or "Shell-i-toes" as my grandma called it), downtown Cincinnati's largest department store. Shopping was a dress-up affair. The bus ride was a necessary evil.

Since most families in our blue-collar neighborhood owned one vehicle, which Dad took to work, the women and children were relegated to public transportation. Buses were hot, smelly and took about an hour for a 15-minute trip. It was the bus that also presented my first ethical dilemma. If you were age 6 or under, the fare was a mere 13-cents. Over age 6, it jumped to an exorbitant 26-cents. My mother, of course, told an 8-year-old me to smile at the driver and say I was 5. I actually knew kids who were 12 and still trying to pass for a kindergartner.

Bus drivers possessed an inordinate amount of power in the 1950s. Not only could they interrogate you about your age, but they could charge double for a transfer if you forgot to ask when you boarded. They also bellowed and cursed when you asked for change. A 6-year-old kid, handing the driver a quarter and saying, "change please" was treated to scowls for the duration of the ride. (Scowls in the rear-view mirror if you sat in the back).

The #21 bus also presented me with an "occasion of sin" a few times on every round trip. As we wound our way through the shadier neighborhoods at the edge of downtown, I began to eagerly look out the window as the Gayiety loomed near. (Once a noted house of burlesque, the Gayiety sank to a cheap strip joint in its waning years.). If luck was with you, a passenger would disembark in front of the Gayiety affording a glimpse of posters for stars such as Ruby Rage or Foxy Faye. "Don't look," my mother would command, as the posters were suggestive and sometimes showed a little too much cleavage for an 8-year-old Catholic girl to witness. The Royal Theater was also on our bus route but was fairly legitimate and only showed soft porn; nothing as daring or sinful as the Gayiety and its lineup of buxom headliners.

Our bus would finally grind to a stinky, smelly halt near the entrance to Shillito's. Always, on the corner where we crossed, was the Pretzel Man. Dressed in a tattered top hat and coordinating accoutrements, the Pretzel Man sold five large dough pretzels for $.25. They were wonderful…still warm and covered with what I think was road salt. We always managed to talk mom into a bag to bring home. My father, who grew up poor, said that when he was hungry, he would eat a bag of dough pretzels and drink a quart of water. The resulting swelling could keep a tummy full for a few days. Later in life, I discovered that those 1950s pretzels were coated in lye to keep them glossy. This could account for many genetic deficiencies in my generation, including reading books by Danielle Steele and buying clothing from Coldwater Creek.

Once inside, we would blissfully travel through the candy department, Pavilion Sportswear, the Miss Shillito Shop and, always, to the perfume department. Here were fashionably-dressed women whose only job was to spray passers-by with Lancôme or Faberge, or hand them a fragrance-soaked piece of blotter paper to tuck in a purse or pocket. True to form, my sister and I would walk in a circle through the department, until we reeked. I think the spray ladies were on to us, but probably thought we were amusing. (After all, they didn't have to ride home on the #21 bus with us)!

Shillito's also taught kids the virtue of patience. Since any whining resulted in no visit to the toy department, we stood for what seemed like hours while our mother tried on hats, dresses, shoes and "foundations." For a period of several months, she visited the fur salon to try on a "scarf" that really consisted of a dead mink with glass eyes, clamping its mouth onto the tail of another dead mink, ad infinitum. It reminded me of wearing your deceased pet chihuahuas to cocktail parties and ladies' luncheons. Her ultimate purchase wound up living in her bedroom closet until furs went out of style. I'd often sneak in a friend or two, unclamp a few of the mouths and do a pretty damn clever ventriloquist act.

We usually ate lunch in the basement, the land of bargains, including food. If mom had come into a windfall, however, she would treat us to the 6th floor Tea Room, the closest I would ever come to touring Versailles. The Tea Room had a real hostess, austere with her hair in a tight knot and menus the size of billboards. Somehow the atmosphere rubbed off as we kids were always on our best behavior. (When in doubt, pinky out)! On a really good day, we'd split the Tea Room's signature dessert…a frozen ball of vanilla ice cream covered in pecans and accompanied by a tiny pitcher of hot fudge. Much as I was tempted to chug the pitcher and devour the ice cream in one bite, decorum won out. I would daintily pour the sauce over the melting dessert and take tiny bites, making it last as long as possible.

Post-lunch was time for the real purpose of our trip. Sometimes it was school shoes, other times it could be winter coats or Easter finery. Once, it was a "sunburst" clock, something my mother had lusted after for months. A few years ago, my sister rescued it and gave it to my daughter, someone who appreciates mid-century modern. Luckily, she didn't give it me or it would have been sold for $2 at a garage sale. I have no taste.

Before our smelly, stinky return trip…and if we had been well-behaved, we were rewarded with a 15-minute stop in the toy department. A true wonderland, especially at Christmas, the department took up half a floor with toys that we could look at, but not buy until a birthday or holiday. (We did not get a random, $20 toy just for our participation). My favorite section was a large endcap with "tricks," like a plastic ice cube with a fly in it, a whoopee cushion, intricate metal puzzles, a fake, bloody eye and a handkerchief that magically changed colors in your hand. Because they were inexpensive, my mother would sometimes let me buy one and I would terrorize our neighborhood with a super-authentic trick!

As we rode home, even hotter in the late-afternoon humidity, I still hoped to catch a glimpse of the Gayiety, this time on the other side of the street, so not as alluring. Deposited back in our own suburban neighborhood, we hiked the couple of blocks from the bus stop, dragging our purchases with us and glad to change back into shorts and t-shirts.

I have read that for brick-and-mortar stores to succeed in today's online shopping environment, they must provide the shopper with an "experience." It seems like we made our own experience. Shopping downtown was somehow thrilling. Enjoying fancy desserts, staring at aisles of toys and playing in our bare feet smelling of Chanel No. 5 is still memorable 60 years later.

Ladies take up the gauntlet! The next time you make a trip to Costco, don your heels, white gloves, pearls and chihuahuas. Make your kids wait for 90 minutes while you search through Kirkland capris and tank tops. Stick your pinky out at the food court and, if you can find a Pretzel Man, eat a bag and drink a quart of water. It'll definitely be an experience!

Limburger Cheese, The Shooting Star and an Ethical Dilemma

What combined the fright of COVID-19, the fun of a birthday party and the anticipation of Christmas? Price Hill Day at Coney Island!

It's not often that kids look forward to waking up at the crack of dawn in the summertime, but on Price Hill Day, my sister and I were awake and dressed by 6 a.m. We piled into our '54 Chevy for the 20-minute trip to (you guessed it) Price Hill. A west-side Cincinnati German neighborhood, Price Hill was where everyone's grandparents lived in the 1950-60s. Like mine, your grandma and grandpa probably lived in one of the hundreds of two-story homes divided into upstairs and downstairs apartments. Known as a "St. Louis," these buildings were as common in Price Hill as Hudepohl Beer and bratwurst. They had large front porches where elderly relatives sat and ate their bratwurst, drank their Hudepohl and listened to the Cincinnati Reds on radio.

But on Price Hill Day at Coney Island, there was no time to sit on the porch. We knew, even as little kids, that it was essential to get to Coney's Picnic Grove by 8 a.m. in order to secure a "spot." The spot consisted of a wood and metal picnic table, hopefully near one of the few grills that had been permanently installed in the picnic area. On an August Wednesday in the 1950s, it was harder to get a "spot" at Coney Island than it was to land a table on Saturday night at Cincinnati's only 5-star restaurant, The Maisonette.

The travelers included my grandparents, with "Pop" at the wheel, my mother, my older sister and me. In retrospect, I think it odd that my Dad never joined us for any momentous childhood occasion. He was always "at work," or "sleeping so he could go from his day job to his night job." He was a phantom figure, bringing home a paycheck (or two), sleeping and working.

With no interstate highway system winding from one side of the city to another, the trip to Coney Island took nearly an hour. Pop drove one and two-lane roads, including the notorious Columbia Parkway, to deliver us to the land of rides, arcade games and the country's largest in-ground swimming pool. My sister and I could barely contain our excitement when we turned onto Kellogg Avenue and took our place in line at the entry gate. The excitement gave way to boredom, however, as it was just 8 a.m. and the rides didn't open until 10. Two hours sitting in a picnic grove, playing in the gravel and endlessly asking, "What time is it?" could take its toll on even the most patient of children.

Picnic Area Patience

As a marketing ploy, Coney Island created "Days" for all of the Cincinnati and Northern Kentucky neighborhoods. By discounting ride tickets and offering free games and prizes for the kids, Coney assured itself of a robust attendance on an otherwise sparsely populated weekday. I think Price Hill Day was the biggest draw. No resident could resist a place to sit, drink beer and let the kids run wild for several hours. Our family was no exception. Pop unpacked his striped cloth bag holding jugs of beer and Limburger Cheese sandwiches by 8:30 a.m. Grandma, who could out-drink him, brought her own jug, several bottles of Barq's Grape and Orange for us kids, and Pepsi for my mother. We also packed lots of food. Blue-collar families in the 1950s didn't buy amusement park food. The price was considered exorbitant. I didn't know that Coney sold food until I was in high school.

At 10 a.m., my sister and I were given $5 and released to the wilds of the park, with the admonition to return to the picnic table when we ran out of money. "Pay one price" was unheard of back then. You bought strips of tickets, priced at $.05/each. A ride on the top coaster, The Shooting Star, set you back six tickets. . . or 30-cents. You could go a few hours on five bucks, especially in Kiddie Land where the rides were cheaper. Looking back with me, do you think it odd that two kids, ages 9 and 5 would be allowed to wonder, unaccompanied, through the State's largest amusement park? Odder still, was our elementary school's "Singers and

Servers Day," when St. Catharine's would unleash two busloads of unchaperoned kids on Coney, telling them to be back to the bus by 6 p.m. It worked. I never heard of a singer or server who missed the ride home, nor did I know of any families that lost a child who had ventured off to ride the Flying Scooters. We knew. Late for the ride home and you faced the consequences of your actions.

Swallowing Your Fear ... And a Barq's Grape

My sister recently confessed to me that what she had passed off as a love of amusement games, was really the fact that the rides scared her. In her early years, she spent most of her time in the "air conditioned" Penny Arcade with an occasional trip to Kiddie Land to ride the Teddy Bear roller coaster and maybe the ponies. It was the Teddy Bear that presented me with yet another childhood ethical dilemma. A roving photographer for The Price Hill News snapped my picture as I sat in the front car of the child-sized wooden coaster. He asked if I lived in Price Hill. I struggled. My grandparents lived in Price Hill, I didn't. Still, if I said no, he would rove further to find a kid who fit the bill and I would lose my 15 minutes of fame, possibly on the front page of this week's issue. My mother would have been proud. . . I lied. My sister still has the yellow copy of the front page, featuring my photo with the caption, "Barbara Lockard, Price Hill resident, enjoys a ride on the Teddy Bear, at Coney Island's Price Hill Day." Fame is a cruel mistress!

At age 11, my sister suddenly became a roller coaster aficionado. Saddled with a 7-year-old younger sibling who still wanted to spend the day in Kiddie Land, she spent Price Hill Day complaining, or trying to cajole me into riding The Wildcat, "just once!" No way, Ray! I was not riding the monstrous wooden coaster. The following year, we paired up with two sisters we met as they argued in the ticket line. Seems their age difference was the same as ours and the younger one was more of a chicken than I was. Sister X and I spent most of the day happily riding in Kiddie Land, until she abruptly decided that we, too, needed to ride The Wildcat. I still don't know what possessed me, as we rode, not only The Wildcat, but also the even more monstrous, Shooting Star. I rode them each once. I never rode or went near them again. I had proven my mettle, impressing my cynical sister, at least for the rest of the day.

Another favorite ride as we grew older, was The Lost River. Starting out with a boat ride through a slightly smelly tunnel, the pullies that dragged the boat, eventually changed angles and began tugging you up a steep hill. You were given just enough time at the top for a throaty scream, before plummeting down and back into the "river," getting pretty wet in the process. My cousin Billy, who was always in trouble, once rocked his boat from side to side so hard that it became wedged in the tunnel. This caused a major back up and when the ride attendants freed his boat, about 10 more boats traveled in tandem up and down the steep precipice. This resulted in a huge round of applause from bystanders who were watching the ride, hoping to catch a splash of water on a hot summer day. As teenagers, guys would come up to you in line and ask if you wanted to ride with them. I always wanted to answer, "Sure, just what I want to do. Ride through a dark tunnel with a guy I don't know!" It was like W.C. Fields who said that he would never belong to any club that would have him for a member. I would never fall for any guy who would ask me to ride on The Lost River with him.

This Ain't No Kiddie Ride!

Tired and sticky, we returned to the picnic table by 7 p.m., grabbing a grilled hot dog before loading into Pop's green, '55 Buick. This is where the true element of terror began. Even with an incredible tolerance for hops, my grandfather could not remain coherent after drinking beer steadily from 8:30 a.m.-7 p.m. (My grandmother, who matched him beer for beer was still pretty sober, but she couldn't drive. My mother could drive but refused to do so on the unfamiliar roads of Cincinnati's east side). From the back seat, we watched in horror as the Buick continually swerved from lane to lane, narrowly missing oncoming traffic. Columbia Parkway, with its high speeds, retaining walls and deceptive curves was worse than the Shooting Star, even though no tickets were required. Somehow, we always managed to make it home, with my mother swearing she would not expose us to this irresponsible driving ever again.

But a year is forgiving, and we didn't miss a Price Hill Day until we were just too old, and too cool to ride the Teddy Bear and white-knuckle it in the back seat of Pop's Buick.

Trick or Treat. Smell My Feet. Give Me Something Good to Eat!

In the 1950s, Halloween night was a free-for-all!

I live in a very conservative part of the world. Over the years, many residents of my northwest Ohio town have spent a lot of energy trying to ban Harry Potter from school libraries; refusing to scan their cards at the local YMCA (the Universal Product Code is intrinsically evil) and never saying, "Happy Holidays!" Just let these folks get within a few months of October 31, though, and they become godless souls, adorning their homes with zombies, demons and gourds. . . lots and lots of gourds. They are, simply put, <u>smitten</u> with Halloween.

Celebrating really begins around the end of August, with Christmas-sized displays of orange lights, giant inflatable Frankenstein's and wooden tombstones strewn about carefully manicured lawns. The biggest event of the fall season (non-COVID times) is a 2-hour long Halloween parade featuring costumed Girl Scouts, local politicians, Shriners in clown cars and high school bands. On trick or treat night, homeowners on South Main Street fortify themselves with bags of Kit-Kats and Smarties, preparing for the 900+ visitors they annually receive.

Even in all of its commercialized splendor, Halloween today is still a short-lived, regimented event. Halloween in the 1950s was a total "experience."

Based on "The Purge," our trick or treat night was uncontrolled and unencumbered by over-zealous adults. Oh sure, parents gave out candy, but that was the extent of their participation. As far as roaming down dark streets, two miles from home, you were on your own.

First rule, or lack thereof, is there was no minimum (or maximum for that matter) age limit. Four-year-old's followed older siblings until they were ditched. Not all, but most, found their way home…or latched on to another nearby bunch of kids. There was no distance limit and no time limit. Trick or treat ended when the last kid was too tired to lug his "booty" any further. As for wandering into strange neighborhoods, it was all part of the adventure. ("But Mom, we KNOW all the serial killers around here!")

Let me emphasize that Halloween was not the "second most profitable holiday" of the marketing calendar back then. Costume choices were limited. You could be a ghost, devil, skeleton or witch. Most were purchased at Woolworth's and consisted of a highly flammable cover-up and a plastic mask. The year my sister needed to be a Dutch Girl for the school play, my dad got out his drafting tools and came up with a creation worthy of Hans Brinker. That Dutch Girl costume was re-purposed until we were teenagers.

There was nothing worse than having a cold Halloween and being ordered to wear a coat or sweater over your costume. We would brave temperatures in the single digits rather than cover up our trick or treat identities. The local grocery didn't carry special trick or treat bags, lights or glow sticks. Most kids grabbed a pillowcase because they didn't tear and had lots of room. If you had used a paper bag, some health nut was bound to throw in an apple and rip the bottom out.

Even though many kids dumped and re-filled their pillowcases three or four times, we were still a "quality over quantity" generation. Big (or nickel) candy bars were the most sought-after. Mini candy bars were tolerated. Apples were thrown away. Well-meaning older women would often hand out homemade doughnuts or cupcakes that wound up smashed at the bottom of a pile of Almond Joys, or, worse, apples.

I recall, back in the 1970s, the City of Cincinnati held trick or treat on Sunday afternoons. This was to combat a rash of harmful foreign objects found in candy. Kids were encouraged ONLY to visit houses where they knew the occupants. Hospitals offered free X-rays of all treats. It was depressing.

Maybe the urge to harm children hadn't emerged yet in the 50s. We unabashedly ate our treats right out of the bag, even if the person giving them to you was a "weirdo." We didn't X-ray appendages, much less candy. I had a friend who broke his leg falling off of a horse and it took his parents three days to give the OK to X-ray his femur. (They would have laughed at doing an MRI of a Hershey Bar).

A retired Navy veteran a few doors away held an annual Halloween night party for his many sailor friends. As the evening wore on, they became pretty inebriated and that's when we attacked. We knew that the guests became more generous the more they drank. They handed out money like... well, like sailors! It wasn't unusual to leave the merriment with several dollar bills. Some years, we'd double-back and the revelers didn't even remember we'd been there earlier. Another round of drinks; another round of dollars!

As liberating as Halloween was, there were still a few of us who for whom trick or treating on foot did not satisfy the wanderlust.

As pre-teens, my sister and a friend talked friend's mother into chauffeuring them to the "rich" part of town over by the country club. Here, they visited a world of embarrassingly long, ranch homes. Walks up the endless driveways proved to be worth it, as they received only nickel candy bars and sometimes entire small bags of treats. When they returned, we gathered around them like novice explorers around Admiral Byrd. They regaled us with tales of a home that actually had an elevator for cars; homes with fountains in the living rooms, and of meeting a real celebrity who hosted Pantomime Hit Parade on local TV! After this, you couldn't keep 'em down on the farm and for several Halloweens thereafter, they would snub their working- class neighborhood for the high life, five miles away.

One of the biggest benefits of being Catholic in the 50s (and this is MY opinion, not doctrine), was that All Saints Day was a "Holy Day of Obligation," which meant school was cancelled. Oh yeah, All Saints Day just happened to be the day after Halloween! Us St. Catharine's kids lulled around in bed, or carefully sorted candy, while our public-school counterparts yawned their way to the 7:30 a.m. school bus. Rumor was that Halloween was the biggest time of year for the Catholic Church to nab "converts." A life of fish on Fridays and foregoing candy during Lent was a good trade-off for being able to sleep in after logging 53 miles schlepping a 40-pound pillowcase while dodging serial killers from the other side of the tracks.

Gosh, I know how much kids like taking advice from old people, so I'll end this with my usual words of wisdom! Children of 2020, heed these words! This Halloween, as you go about collecting your gluten-free, nut-free, safety-tested treats, enjoy the "fun scary" that comes with believing just a little in goblins, witches, haunted houses and candy bars with no nutritional value. Relish the goosebumps that appear when you turn down that darkened alley. (So what if it's right behind your house?) Take your little brother or sister with you, even though it's a drag, and watch a creepy movie after your scheduled candy-hustling time is over. The more you let yourself experience "fun scary" the less frightening 2020's "real scary" will be!

Purgatory, Disinfectant and Communists

Corona virus no match for 1950s nuns!

If this pandemic had occurred in the 1950s, St. Catharine Elementary School on the west side of Cincinnati would have remained open. The good sisters who comprised 98% of the school's faculty would have told students to "offer it up" and, if you were unfortunate enough to succumb to the virus, you could be a martyr for your faith. Our nuns loved martyrs, almost as much as they hated the communists.

Had it been available, they would have seen online instruction as a communist plot. (It would be so easy for Nikita Khrushchev to hack the school's website and present himself as an instructor of math and authority on the Baltimore catechism). St. Catharine's nuns blamed communism for every perceived evil in the world. Staunch supporters of Joe McCarthy, they described "the communists" to a group of frightened first-graders as something resembling a cross between the creature from Predator and a plate of Olive Garden calamari.

In the 8th grade, upon reading a definition of communism in the glossary of a library book, I experienced something close to the rapture. The book defined communism as a "political and economic system." A system? No beasts with tentacles busting into your classroom and demanding that you spit on the crucifix? No army of little, bald men banging their size-6 shoes on a table screaming, "We will bury you?" It was just a system. Nothing very frightening to a kid of 13.

My elementary school teachers were also big fans of social distancing; not because of possible droplet-borne pathogens, but because bad behavior could be transmitted if you sat near someone with sinful habits. The sisterhood conspired to socially ostracize Teddy P. for all eight grades. His transgression? Teddy ate crayons. From age 6-12, he enjoyed a few fine Crayolas every morning, munching happily on a cerulean or periwinkle oblivious to Sr. Julian's threats of extended time in Purgatory.

What was it about Purgatory that made it frightening, but sort of a tame punishment considering it ultimately ended with a trip to heaven? True, time spent could total 2.5 million years, but much preferable to the eternity of hell. (The concept of eternity kept me awake nights, tossing and turning for what seemed like an eternity). Ah, but there was a catch for getting probation in purgatory… a plenary indulgence.

Catholic children could "earn" indulgences for good works, like saying the Hail Mary 20 times, or writing "JMJ" at the top of your homework papers. Each indulgence was redeemable for so many days off of your purgatorial sentence. A plenary, however, was like a "Get Out of Jail FREE" card. A plenary indulgence wiped out ALL of your time in Purgatory, allowing you to go speedily to the pearly gates.

As an adult, my grown-up mind realized the poor logic behind allowing sinful Catholics to earn more than one plenary indulgence. So let me get this right … you could get out of Purgatory an unlimited amount of times? Sort of like purchasing 10 lifetime memberships to Planet Fitness. One is probably good enough!

Lest you think it irresponsible of our 50s counterparts to keep school in session during a national emergency, keep in mind the nuns' secret weapon…disinfectant. Classrooms, hallways and even students were disinfected daily with a solution that smelled a little like formaldehyde and a little like the noodle soup that cooked continually in our small cafeteria. (The noodle soup alone could have eradicated COVID-19). The sisters knew that no virus could withstand an army of habit-clad soldiers armed with glass bottles and sponges. High performing students were often chosen to help, proudly puffing out their chests while spraying down classmates.

As we struggle through this current crisis, let's pause a minute to pay tribute to the indomitable spirit of our 1950s nuns. They would have attacked the coronavirus in much the same way they attacked communism and their own crayon-eating charges. Working alongside them, we could even have earned a few indulgences!

We Don't Need No Education. . . in Saddle Shoes

With Apologies to Pink Floyd!

Don't get me wrong. The older I get, the more I sort of like school uniforms. Oh, I still think they're a plot to kill individualism, but the kids <u>do</u> look nice. At any rate, uniforms sure beat tank tops, distressed skinnies and Poison Youth t-shirts.

Let me add that today's options aren't uniforms, but "ensembles." So you actually get a choice among khakis, white shirts, blue shirts, long sleeves or polos, skirts or skorts, or even a cardigan when it's chilly?

"We've got trouble my friends, right here in Ohio. Trouble with a capital *T*, that rhymes with *C* and that stands for choice!"

Back in the day, our nuns knew better than to present kids and adolescents with a choice. Why, that could lead to "choosing" the sinful path rather than the righteous!

I lied. In my west side Cincinnati elementary school, girls actually were given two choices when it came to uniforms; a navy-blue jumper and white blouse, OR a white blouse and navy-blue jumper. (Decisions! Decisions!). The shoe of no-choice was the saddle shoe; not only a foot covering, but also a weapon. A single shoe could top the scales at 6 pounds. (There was a time in 4th grade when my shoes equaled one-fourth of my body weight). At St. Catharine's Elementary, the BMI calculation included shoe weight.

Oh yes, uniforms were supposed to be the great equalizer. The poor kids would not bear the stigma of having an inferior wardrobe. Everyone would be the same. Ha! The rich kids wore $45 Spaulding's and us poor wretches were forced into black and white plastic imitations with soles made out of vanilla wafers. A pair of poor-kid shoes lasted approximately two months.

In the sixth grade, our Nun Fashion Board decided that a switch to a green plaid jumper with a natty red snap-on tie would boost the collective morale of all the girls at St. Kate's. The jumpers resembled the costume worn by the creature that carried Adrienne Barbeau out of the muck in "Swamp Thing." At least we fared better than a neighboring school where the jumpers hung straight down from the shoulders with no defined waist. This creation left all of the elementary school students looking like itty-bitty unwed mothers.

Through some act of divine intervention, Huber's Department Store in Price Hill received the franchise for all the Catholic school uniforms in our area. (It was either divine intervention, or Huber's had the 4-1-1 on the archbishop)! I believe uniforms were the store's only source of income aside from housedresses and men's undershirts. The Kardashian's would have shunned Huber's.

Most families bought only one uniform per student that was worn five days a week for nearly 10 months each year. Eventually, the uniforms were see-thru, not because they were sexy, but the material had worn so thin that your half-slip was visible. High school saw the retro move back to navy-blue jumpers and white blouses. The only change was a pleated waist and side zipper. Herein lay my sophomore year downfall.

In a hurry to get to school one morning, I broke the zipper on my jumper, rendering it unwearable. Always a quick thinker, I found a navy-blue pleated skirt and paired it with my cheap saddles and stylish navy-blue knee socks. Oh the naivete'! Who was I to think I could run the gauntlet of nuns at Mother of Mercy without being recognized as non-compliant? My demise reminded me of the scene in "Invasion of the Body Snatchers" when the entire town points to the last remaining human being and rats him out!

I didn't even make it through first period, when I was sent to the principal's office and given a loaner jumper. At the time I weighed about 115 lbs. The jumper was a size 42 Woman's. An invitation to my best friend Patty seemed to be in order. We ran into the third-floor girls' room and both of us donned the jumper, standing back-to-back and looking like a set of uber-Catholic Siamese twins. We then strolled down the hall, much to the delight of our classmates. Oh, did I neglect to tell you that our nuns had no sense of humor? They doled out so many demerits to Patty and me that it shattered the previous record set by Marie, who had driven our algebra teacher to hysterical tears in freshman year.

A decade ago, I served on the Findlay City Schools board of education. At one point, some parents suggested we look into uniforms for our high school students. My son, then a junior, told me he would change his name and disown me if I voted in favor of this move toward "uniformity." I tried to convince him of all the advantages; flattering styles, more time to focus on academics, cost savings? What about the memories of joining your friends in the same, extra-large outfit? None of these arguments worked, so I didn't press the issue and uniforms at the high school died a relatively quick death. Oh well. All in all, it's just another brick in the wall.

A Paper Bag, Black Lace and a PBJ: the 50s School Experience

Back in the day, returning to school required good hair and upper body strength!

No one said that school isn't tough for kids in 2020. My 3rd-grade granddaughter returned to a "hybrid" classroom last week. She's with her teacher and 11 fellow students two days a week; in an online synchronous classroom the other three days, with some asynchronous education time thrown in. The kids wear masks, have to socially distance and get about three minutes to eat lunch. Teachers are expected to instruct, maintain hygiene, direct traffic at the end of the day and keep the students stress-free when most adults are at home in a fetal position trying to get a refill for Ativan.

Even with a school year that's a "sh- t show," today's kids still have high expectations for curriculum, fashion, lunch bags and what are considered the essentials for achieving a quality elementary school education. In 1958, in Sr. Julianne's third-grade class, the bar was set pretty low on what you really needed for a successful and "blessed" school year.

I watch students parade out of my granddaughter's school weighed down with a Chrome Book and a Hydraflask. The slim tablet holds a year's worth of text, videos and interactive games in one measley-byte of storage. The owner's only responsibility is to keep it charged and remembering to take it back and forth to school.

Volumes and Volumes

We had six or seven textbooks with an average weight of four pounds each. It took 800 pages to get enough religious doctrine and vocabulary words into a Weekly Reader. Alas, the student's responsibility included keeping the text in good condition, which entailed the dreaded book cover duty.

Book covers were oversized sheets of brown kraft paper, shamelessly printed with ads from the donating sponsor. For as long as I can remember, our covers were provided thanks to the largesse of a local funeral home. I proudly carried a geography book emblazoned with, "When life comes to an end, WE are your friend." The day before the first day of school, kids met in their classrooms and were required to cover all of their books before being allowed to leave (or progress to the next level of their education).

Following the directions on the covers took the skill of a plastic surgeon and the dexterity of an origami master. I had neither, and took the annual prize for the only student who stays at school past dinner and well into the bedtime hour. Once, I had all of my books meticulously covered by 3 p.m., when I was informed that one not only had to have the corners of the volume covered, but the edges of the hard cover as well. Sr. Omar watched in delight as I ripped off all of the covers and started over. Mom had to re-warm dinner several times that night!

Caroline and I spent entire days this past summer, searching for just the right combination of backpack and plutonium-lined lunch bag. She finally settled on matching black and rainbow Addida satchels. The Chrome Book nestles neatly into the backpack, while the lunch bag holds cold packs, hot packs, and could probably accommodate a mini-microwave.

WE toted lunch in a brown paper bag, or in one of those metal contraptions complete with thermos. The metal lunch boxes were usually themed with a Saturday morning cartoon character, or The Lone Ranger for boys. I did learn that a thermos is not a good container for chicken noodle soup. The broth pours out, but the noodles pack together and dangle limply from the opening like some creature who's preparing to battle Sigourney Weaver. A thermos was only good for contraband Coca-Cola or KoolAid. Lunch of choice was usually a PBJ or something that didn't require refrigeration. Cold packs hadn't been invented yet and, even if they had, would not have survived a morning in the 85-degree "cloak room."

Not orthopedically-aware enough for backpacks, we lugged something that resembled a cheap briefcase in one hand. The nuns referred to it as a "book bag," even though our books were too large and too plentiful to fit inside. Walking home usually required lugging a 40 lb. school bag in one hand while tucking another 40 pounds of books into the crook of your elbow on the other arm.

No! Not the Beauty School!

Girls in 2020 return to school with silky hair fresh from a Malibu treatment to remove the summer's chlorine residue. First-graders are treated to balayage and ombre, compliments of one of the many urban spas, plentiful even here in rural northwest Ohio.

We got <u>haircuts.</u>

On Cincinnati's west side in 1958, the salons of choice were Don Seta or (ulp!) the Beauty School. (If I had a Haunted House font, I would utilize it to express how I felt about the Beauty School). Located upstairs of a candy store in Cheviot, Ohio, the Western Hills Academy of Beauty Culture provided haircuts for a dollar or two with a complimentary stint under the hairdryer. Please understand that a lucky few of us emerged with a reasonable, almost cute "do." Entrusting the semi-frizzy, cowlick-laden hair of kids like me to 15-year old Miss Yvonne was a recipe for tonsorial disaster, however.   My hair would have challenged Vidal Sassoon, much less someone who had failed Layer Cuts 101. Luckily, in elementary school, I had not yet developed the adolescent vanity that would have kept me at home until the "trim" grew out. I water-slicked back my hair and carried on. I had bigger fish to fry.

Just as the kids of 2020 cherish their logo-wear, $150 hair color, four-course packed lunches and a year's curriculum stored in something smaller than a Trapper-Keeper, us 50s students also had essentials that saw us through from September to June. For me, these were a chapel veil (a mysterious circlet of black lace that when affixed to a girl's head, assured her that she was worthy to enter the House of the Lord), a St. Joseph's Daily Missal ($3.75 for the cheap version and $6.75 for the leather-bound, deluxe edition), Lives of the Saints, rubber or plastic snow boots, Totes shoe covers (yes, you walked to school in the rain) and a plastic raincoat (I had a boy's Davey Crockett purchased at Robert Hall). This was all topped off with a scapula. The best way to describe a scapula is two squares of cloth connected by something that resembled a shoelace. This was slipped over the head and grasped or kissed often. Scapula were holy relics. They were touched by someone who had touched someone who had touched someone who had touched the coffin of a saint. A good scapula was hard to come by.

September will forever hold for me the trauma of cutting book covers with a dull scissors, the shock and awe of discovering you had scored a favorite teacher, the melancholy of knowing your days of reading comic books under a tree in the backyard were over (at least for 9 months), and the pride of walking the half-mile home for lunch all by yourself. I hope today's kids can overcome the anomaly that's 2020 and retain some positive memories that are just as lasting.

Memories (and Maybe Cures) Are Made of This

What sustained us as kids may be what it takes to knock out COVID-19!

Say what you want about us old folks (You know, the "vulnerable" population). We may be flabby, forgetful and frightened, but we survived some shit in our day! Try playground equipment made of cast iron and built over asphalt. Or, what about riding to Florida lying on the shelf at the base of the rear windshield, laughing hysterically every time Dad hit the brakes and you rolled onto the backseat floor? Many of us also experienced near-suffocation in the car trunk, avoiding the $.75/child admission charge for the local drive-in movie.

Does the fact that we're still here have something to do with the substances we ingested while growing up? Could those same sticky, sugary, chemical-infused necessities of childhood have had some medicinal qualities that rendered us semi-immortal? If we repeated the "dosage" as older adults could we somehow better resist COVID-19?

After much research using peer-reviewed sources (like Life Magazine and TV Guide) I've honed the list of my own childhood talismans to the following:

Lik-M-Aid

Imagine the most germ-laden, diabetic-coma-inducing snack you can think of and you've at least got the concept. A small envelope of brightly colored sugar with the words, "It's Fun to Eat" on the front, Lik-M-Aid was shaken onto a dirty palm and licked off, hopefully by the owner of said hand. Not only did the user get a sugar high, but a bacteria high as well, since the vector had also been pressed into service that day to wipe a little brother's nose, squish a few insects and turn a dirty jump rope. Of course, before Lik-M-Aid goes into clinical trials, scientists would have to get the hand toxins right. It's that delicate combination of germs, sugar and preservatives that just may deliver a one-two punch to the old coronavirus. A reminder that this is the original, 1950s Lik-M-Aid and not that wimpy-ass "Fun Dip" made by Wonka in the 90s. (Fun Dip had a spoon for God's sake!)

First Friday Rolls

To assure accuracy, I must add that this could be a regional therapeutic, as the real First Friday rolls were a product of Montana Bakery, Cheviot, Ohio. The backstory… Catholics in the 1950s could jump through all kinds of hoops to earn their way out of near eternal damnation. (See my post on Plenary Indulgences.). If a member of the faith, child or adult, took communion on nine consecutive first Fridays of the month, he or she earned a lifetime pass out of Purgatory, a place where you burned just like in Hell, but it was temporary, so endured cheerfully. We were never told why the magic number was nine, but eight First Fridays wouldn't get you out of the fourth grade much less Purgatory.

This being pre-John XXIII, even kids were required to fast for three hours before taking communion. Since we attended Mass at 8 a.m., this meant not eating breakfast. While you were allowed to bring soggy doughnuts or Hostess cupcakes for an in-school snack, on First Fridays you could order rolls delivered to your classroom…and oh, what rolls they were! Consisting of greasy dough covered with sugary icing, laced with a sugary red jam substitute, two-for-a quarter First Friday rolls could sustain a child through a semester of elementary school. If eaten during today's pandemic, the grease would most certainly protect your mucous membranes from infection. If not, COVID-19 would die from hypoglycemia.

Velveeta

Yes, it's still around today, but this "cheese food" is not the diet staple it was in the mid-20th century. We were Velveeta purists, eating hunks of the stuff to stave off starvation in the hours before lunch or supper. With its strange, gelatinous texture, you could squish and mold Velveeta into various shapes before popping it in your mouth and enjoying the bland but satisfying taste. My mother would pack us Velveeta sandwiches for lunch, while my father kept a cube in his toolbox as sort of an all-purpose patching material. Rumor had it that if you squeezed Velveeta hard enough it would drip. Never had any luck proving this. Would it help ward off a pandemic viral invasion? Maybe not, but offering it to potential guests might just encourage more social distancing.

French Chew

The seriousness of COVID-19 might just warrant the ultimate weapon in our childhood arsenal; a real Doomsday Machine…the French Chew. The words "French Chew" struck fear in my mother's heart like no other cavity-creating substance could. We'd come home from the community pool, covered in mercurochrome, band-aids and bee stings and the only thing my mother would yell at us was, "You didn't have a French Chew, did you?" She hated the slabs of vanilla, strawberry or chocolate taffy coated in powdered sugar as much as we loved them. French Chews "pulled your fillings out." Fillings cost money. Ergo, French Chews were banned.

In my estimation, my mother's indictment of the French Chew was unjust. The candy bar had more adhesive power than Super Glue. If they had had enough French Chews on the Titanic. the crew could have easily repaired the gash in the ship's hull and continued on to New York safely. Someone told me of a kid who could eat a frozen French Chew, but this was akin to chewing roofing tar that had been left outside during the month of January in Ohio. While probably not a cure for the coronavirus, French Chews could be the ultimate PPE. A Chew carried in the mouth while out in public would attract and trap any germ-laden particle that dared to come your way.

So while, I'm still adhering to the 6-foot rule, wearing a mask and washing my hands every three seconds, I'm going to press some of my childhood sustainers into service. The next time you see me, I might have purple lips, orange palms, missing teeth and chubby cheeks from stashed wads of cheese food…but I'll be healthy!

The Silver Lining May Just be Yellow Stamps

Stamps gave us hope, dreams and lamps.

Not exactly cheerful times we're living in. There's a global pandemic, protests, murder hornets, fires in California, hurricanes in Florida and the start of the political TV commercial season. Mental health experts warn of a second pandemic; one with symptoms of depression, anxiety and crying jags. What can we cling to that promises a light at the end of the tunnel? Is there a cure. . . a vaccine as it were, for helplessness, hopelessness and a dearth of dreams?

As kids, no matter how bad things got, (yes, we had the threat of nuclear war, the Cuban Missile Crisis and "Car 54 Where Are You?") we were dreamers. Those dreams were fueled by toy catalogs at Christmas, Harry & David at Easter, and the Top Value Stamp Redemption Book the rest of the year. Today's kids get immediate gratification with Amazon one-click or an Apple Wallet stuffed with digital cash by loving parents. We had ample dreaming time while saving enough Top Value Stamps to get a transistor radio or a bonnet hairdryer. We were simple folk with simple wants.

Lick 'Em and Stick 'Em

Shoppers received trading stamps at the cash register of their local grocery stores and redeemed them for a plethora of gifts, ranging from the mundane (a 2-slice toaster) to the magnificent (an in-ground swimming pool). There were a variety of stamp brands, but in Cincinnati, the most popular was the Top Value Stamp. The yellow strips of stamps, earned at your neighborhood Kroger store, were your ticket to material wealth, or, at least, a classy floor lamp. My research tells me that one stamp was issued for each 10-cents spent. We were too naïve to know that the stores that offered stamps also had higher prices. Our families paid dearly for those crockpots and Timex watches.

Lest you think that "stamp collecting" was strictly a mercenary pastime, I remind you that, what was basically a brand promotion, contributed to family togetherness and true cooperation between parent and child. We spent many nights at the kitchen table, either licking or rubbing the backs of stamps with a wet paper towel and placing them carefully in a savings book. After a few years, some retail genius decided to make larger stamps worth 10 or 50 of the single stamps. This cut down considerably on sticking time and helped alleviate the national saliva shortage.

As a sign of respect, mothers had first choice on redemption store finery. The gift was usually something to benefit the entire family, like a steam iron or alarm clock. My mother once treated herself to a cloth laundry cart to wheel around the backyard. There was even a pocket for clothespins. (Mom's head was always turned by luxury items). I always hoped to save enough Top Values for a pony. There he was, right in the book, complete with western saddle and bridle; a pinto pony for just 150 books of yellow stamps!

There were no abstracts back then. There was no online ordering or bitcoins. You lugged books of stamps to the redemption center where clerks diligently paged through each one to make sure there were no blank pages. There were even "half book" denominations requiring the clerk to tear a book in half and give you a half back to use for future redemptions. Something about physically touching your "cash" made your purchase all the more valuable. I think the Top Value stamp is responsible for my Scrooge McDuck theory of wealth. I don't want to invest my money or put it into an IRA. I just want to swim through cash, diamonds, rubies and gold in a pool in my mansion. This is probably why I'll be working until I'm 96.

What's in a Name?

Different from stamps, but with the same dream quotient, were contests. I spent about two years of my life trying to come up with the winning name for a racehorse being offered as first prize in a contest sponsored by a chewing tobacco company. I had the perfect name, if those judges would just read my entries. I would fly up the sidewalk of Eggers Place on a steed known as "Volcanic Ash." Where I would keep a 16-hand thoroughbred on our $1/10^{th}$-acre lot in Westwood remained to be determined.

My prize quest was always equine in nature. Comic books in the 50s and 60s lured kids as young as six to sell Cloverine Brand Salve. This was actually a pyramid scheme where adults made off with the cash and hardworking kids earned points redeemable for prizes. The grand prize, and this is the god's honest truth, was a live monkey! Even a cute capuchin, however, couldn't dissuade me from my goal of winning that pinto pony. (I wonder how long he stuck around before some kid won him on their way to monkey glory)? The ingredients of Cloverine Band Salve were petroleum jelly, rectified turpentine and white wax. In 1967, the Federal Trade Commission put the ka-bosh on the Wilson Chemical Company using juveniles to hawk their wares; the end of a glorious era of entrepreneurship!

Ironically, even though she had never set foot in a barn, a schoolmate who lived about three blocks from me won the Edsel Pony! For you young'uns, the Edsel represented Ford Motor Company's attempt to market the car of the future. Between 1958-60, Ford lost $250 million on the Edsel and the name has become synonymous with "commercial failure."

The name-the-pony contest was Edsel's desperate attempt to attract attention to what really was a damned ugly car! My friend has chosen the banal name of "Pokey," for the dapple-gray pony that was delivered to her postage-stamp sized backyard one afternoon. As we kids lined up for rides, I was still dumfounded that such an unimaginative choice had warranted my friend a coveted prize. I mean, Pokey was no "Volcanic Ash". I learned later that the winner's father had purchased a new Edsel a week prior, so comforted myself with the thought that the contest was rigged. As it was, Pokey only spent a few days in our neighborhood before he was trailered off to a nearby farm.

I've come the long way around to my theory that we need more Edsel Ponies, more Cloverine Brand Salve and definitely more Top Value Stamps to keep our kids' ability to dream alive. Dreams can't be undermined by shut-downs, shelter in place orders and shower curtains between school desks. After all, isn't the definition of an optimist someone who runs through a barn full of manure shouting, "There's a pony in here somewhere!"

We all need to keep looking for that pony.

Why I'm Bat Shit Crazy. . . And so Are You (Probably)

1950s parents and teachers weren't exactly easy on the psyche!

(Having served two terms on our local board of education, I became all too familiar with the term, "trauma informed learning." This approach has become necessary in our 2020 classrooms because so many of our students have suffered or are suffering from trauma in their lives. Our teachers and administrators do a phenomenal job in this environment and I continue to wish them good fortune and supported tax levies)!

As always, I can't help but compare today's teaching and parenting philosophies with that of my own parents and the good sisters at my Catholic elementary school. In the 50s, aside from being lower middle-class and living with 10 siblings in a two-bedroom, one bath house, most of us didn't have much trauma in our lives. My parents, like many others of that era, practiced "trauma-induced learning," or, "I'll give you something to cry about!" My mom, in particular, took the easy route to discipline; resorting to threats, myths and lies to achieve a well-behaved child. Our teachers, most of whom were 75-year-old nuns, one-upped parents by relying on urban legends, apocalyptic predictions and an occasional tale of torture. Consider that all of this was delivered by a large woman in a black and white costume that looked like it came from Hammer Studios, and you had to give the nuns the disciplinary advantage.

The child-rearing theories of the 1950s produced us. . . a hard-working, conscientious generation that is also crazy as hell. Tell me one person you know who doesn't suffer from anxiety, depression, bi-polar disorder, agoraphobia or compulsive something. Reaching back into my subconscious, I have managed to pinpoint specific parent/teacher strategies that are probably responsible for my emotional instability. (I put on a good front, though)!

"Hello, Girls Town?"

Located in Hamilton County, Ohio, Girls Town (of the Good Shepherd) was an orphanage and reform school for delinquent or pregnant girls. Although I had never seen the actual facility, my mother explained to my sister and me that Girls Town was a place where parents could send their wayward daughters for infractions ranging from not picking up their toys, to whining during their mothers' endless phone conversations. Now, being a particularly surly child, I often drove my mom beyond human endurance, especially on days when my dad was working a double shift. She had an easy fix. She would stroll over to our black, party-line telephone, pick up the receiver and say loudly, "Hello Girls Town? I have a bad girl here and want you to come and get her!"

I was strong-willed, but the Girls Town calls would cause me to crumble into a sorry heap at my mother's feet, crying and begging her not to send me away. I would be good, I blubbered. I would sit and read Golden Books while she talked for three hours with her friend, Virginia. Name your poison, Mom. You had me at "Hello".

Mom also had a few other tried and true threats in her disciplinary bag. A favorite was warning me that if I went outside in my ballet leotard, a policeman would come and arrest me. I was terrified of the police (which was ironic considering my father was a cop). This was actually a ploy to keep me from playing outside in my dance gear and wearing it out. That stuff cost money, so the lie was justified in Mom's way of thinking. One day, however, while I was playing indoors in my tutu, my mother had to leave the house in a hurry and tried to herd my sister and me into the car. I lie on the floor screaming that I had to change clothes or would be arrested. This caused a 20-minute delay in her departure. Paybacks are hell!

Frozen Arms and Eternity

Scholars tell us that fairy tales were written to scare disobedient children into submission. Well, our nuns must have taken a page from Hans

Christian Anderson, because they began each school day with a frightening tale, bound to keep you on the straight and narrow. Lifting her eyes heavenward, Sister Angeline, our principal, would recount the story of a young boy who was disrespectful to his mother, to the point of threatening to strike her. "And as Tommy pulled back his arm to hit his dear mother, God froze his arm in that position forever!" Such was also the case with Alice, who used a swear word at dear old mom, and holy water began cascading from her mouth.

Eternity was a complex and equally frightening topic. A friend told me that one of his elementary school nun's stories involved a dove flying around an earth-sized ball of pure steel. Once, during each trip around the globe, the dove's wing would brush against the ball of steel. "The time it takes for that dove to wear away the entire steel ball is just a fraction of what eternity means. . . and eternity is how long you will burn in hell if you commit a mortal sin." (Bat shit crazy, I swear)!

Here's to Little Jimmy, Wherever You Are!

The problem with us Catholics is that we won't tolerate complaining, resulting in lots of repressed anger and the desire to occasionally slap people silly. Throughout childhood, our kvetching would be met with responses like, "Offer it up," or (again) "I'll give you something to cry about!" For Mom, there was "Little Jimmy." Looking back, I doubt there was such a person, but depending on the situation, Little Jimmy suffered maladies ranging from having no limbs, to having limbs that were paralyzed, to having OK limbs, but being visually impaired, etc. We would whine about having a headache and Mom would immediately retort, "How dare you complain when you could be Little Jimmy!"

A few years ago when my son was visiting from college, he happened to get a bad haircut and mentioned it during a dinner with my mother. Boy, was she ready! She had been waiting for years to drag Little Jimmy out of mothballs. "John, how can you complain about a haircut when you could be Little Jimmy?" (My son whispered to me that he didn't see how his bad hair day had anything to do with a fictitious child who had no limbs. Hey, who said a university education isn't worth it?)

Another one of Mom's snappy retorts was, "I complained because I didn't have any shoes and then I met a man who didn't have any feet." Now this may have been a good maxim to shut up a couple of crying kids, but let me tell you, if my mother didn't have any shoes, the entire world would have heard about it. She was the Imelda Marcos of west side Cincinnati. Never one to soldier through adversity, Mom talked a good game. To this day, though, neither my sister, nor I ever want to admit we're not feeling up to par. "COVID-19? No, no, I'm fine. Just a little tickle in the throat!"

There were other guilt-producing ploys that still haunt me and are probably responsible for thousands of dollars spent on Freudians, Jungians and Mogen-Davidians. About twice a week, my mom would remind me that because I was such a large baby, I tilted her gallbladder which caused her many months of pain and a (then) lengthy surgery. One of the nuns' favorites, usually delivered when you were in an otherwise great mood, is describing the Pope crying when he read the letter from Our Lady of Fatima. (Did she predict the cancellation of Battle Star Galactica? The 2020 presidential election? Pinterest?)

O.K., get ready for some FREE therapy! If I've learned one thing in my nearly seven decades, it's that complaining (whining and kvetching) is warranted and completely legit. If you feel badly about something, even if it's a "First World problem," then FEEL bad! Don't think about martyrs, missionaries, eternity, biting on a bullet or holding back tears. By all means, keep your compassion for others, but have lots and lots of compassion for yourself. Buy yourself a present. Treat yourself to a double chocolate doughnut at Tim Horton's, or keep avoiding that chore you've been putting off. Contrary to popular opinion, wallowing in self-pity is highly underrated! Give it a try!

Thoughts and General Comments on the Present-Day Insanity!

Why It Sucks to be Old During a Pandemic

It's not just higher risk, it's the other shit!

First, let me say that I <u>am</u> an old person. I am not hanging on the beach at Cabo with my spring break cronies, thumbing my nose at the health risks I may be bringing home to my grandma. In addition to being old, I have an underlying medical condition…because, face it, who do you know over age 65 that does NOT have an underlying medical condition? (This is based on the study published in JAMA and presented at several Pampered Chef parties, titled, "Once You Pass 50, Your Body Turns into Expired Taco Meat Wrapped in Skin").

I'm building a case for my credibility in listing some, perhaps heretofore unmentioned reasons, that being old not only sucks, but being old during a pandemic sucks big time. Please join me in the litany of cruel tricks that a pandemic plays on us oldsters:

You are "vulnerable." Duh! Of course, we're vulnerable. We've got high everything…BP, cholesterol and sugar. While your grandchildren may get a case of the sniffles and your kids might spend a day or two under the weather, if you're north of 65, you'll need to hold a bake sale to buy a ventilator. Luckily, some of us are still savvy enough to outfox the germs and the rest of us are pretty good bakers.

The special "senior hours" at local discount stores aren't so special. Why is it that America thinks all senior citizens wake up at dawn, just chomping at the bit to push a cart down aisles brimming with everything but the essentials? (During the height of the toilet paper shortage in March, my husband was thrilled to see that there was still plenty of gefelte fish available). The stores also don't give you a lot of time to get the hell out of Dodge before a younger, germier clientele arrives. Seniors are lucky if they get an hour to shop, and again, this is usually between 4-5 a.m.

Most of us look like hell in Zoom meetings. Last week, I attended a Zoom meeting with six, 30-year-olds. Cezanne would have depicted the meeting in a still life as six, fleshy robust apples surrounding a prune. Matisse may have portrayed it as six beautiful vases brimming with flowers, standing upright next to a withered stalk of celery. I spend the better part of online get-togethers searching in vain for a wrinkle or other facial flaw on the other attendees. Q: What's a "Baby Zoomer?" A: Someone who wears their COVID mask to online meetings.

We need to cultivate a fear of germs. Just about everyone born before 1955 grew up with the "5-second rule." For the uninitiated, this is when you drop food on the floor and have 5 seconds to pick it up and (safely) eat it. Houses were built with one bathroom and an occasional lone toilet located in the basement. Families with eight kids, one bathroom and three bedrooms were the norm in our Catholic school. You didn't get a lot of opportunities to wash your hands and a weekly bath was considered good hygiene. Hand sanitizer? Wha'??? If we got a cut or scrape, my dad said to, "Let a dog lick it." Everyone knew that dog saliva had magic, medicinal properties. This advice was from the same dad who once removed a bone chip from his elbow with a paperclip. (Of course, he held the paperclip over a lit match to "sterilize" it. This was the most important step prior to self-surgery of any type).

The technology needed to exist during a pandemic in 2020 eludes us. C'mon, some of us just got the hang of email and now we're expected to change our virtual backgrounds on Zoom and download an app for COVID-19 testing. I understand that actor Woody Harrelson is tweeting that symptoms of coronavirus are really a reaction to radiation from 5g. Personally, I think it's radiation emanating from flip phones, which is why seniors are more vulnerable, which takes us back to the beginning of this blog.

Here in Ohio, there are some advantages to being old. We get "Golden Buckeye" discounts and cheaper entrance fees to State parks. Those who like dinner at 3 p.m. can show up for early-bird meals and we get programs with adorable names like, "Silver Sneakers". Still, I think I'd rather spend more and be 30. My chances in battling COVID-19 would be improved and I sure as hell would look better in a still life!

Sticks and Stones. . . and Pumpkins?

Hey Boomers! Tired of being patronized?

Why is it that the more prestigious and highly rated healthcare organizations are usually those that have facilities resembling a Rural King or Mattress Warehouse? Although this article is intended to address patronizing language toward older adults, I find it necessary to set the stage with a vivid description of a trip to Columbus to visit an Ohio healthcare giant.

So two years ago, I traveled to this big box store of health for a cardiac MRI, something that apparently was not available in my small northwest Ohio city. I wound my way through massive construction (there is always construction that is NEVER completed) to the radiology area which had been spared any renovation since, perhaps, 1955. The lighting was dim. I was handed a torn plastic bag for my personal belongings and discovered that one of the two restrooms was not functioning. After sitting in a colorless waiting area for 20 minutes, I was summoned by a nurse to one of the many small prep rooms.

Having worked in healthcare for most of my life, I have the utmost respect for nurses. This particular nurse seemed extremely competent, taking my health history, drawing blood and answering my questions. All was well until she said, "O.K., Pumpkin, I'll wheel you into the MRI." I did a double-take. Had this healthcare professional just addressed me as a large, orange vegetable? As we approached the room with the magnet, she did it again. "I'll come and get you when you're done and you can get dressed, Pumpkin." By now, I really needed that cardiac MRI and almost called her out on her endearing term. (Calling out someone who is sticking needles into your veins and has your plastic bag of clothing locked up somewhere required more courage than I had, however).

I reported this inappropriate manner of addressing patients on the six-page survey of my treatment that the major Ohio healthcare provider had sent by email. Never got a response. Guess they don't take pumpkins seriously. It started me thinking, though, would this otherwise professional nurse have addressed a 30-year-old guy as "Pumpkin"? Would she have addressed any male patient as anything but "sir" or by his first name? Unfortunately, older women seem to be the targets of elderspeak, and sometimes the culprits are older men themselves!

Young at Heart . . . Bullshit!

Older men, from Wal-Mart greeters to bank tellers, have referred to me as "Young Lady." C'mon, I'm not infirm, and I don't drool, but I am definitely NOT a young lady. It's sort of like calling someone who is obviously overweight, "Slim". In the future, I have vowed that I am going to respond to every incidence of being called a "Young Lady," with, "Thanks, Old Fart!"

We have a well-stocked local drugstore that I have stopped patronizing because, as soon as I crossed the threshold, the manager would shout out for everyone to hear, "Oh, honey, do you need help?" Now, while I may need help dealing with a changing world, or the sticky ignition on my truck, I do NOT need help finding deodorant. It's like when you're asked, "Do you need help out with that?" when your package consists of gum and a bottle of hair gel. I am always tempted to respond, "No, but where are you when I'm trying to load the 100 lb. bag of Blue Buffalo into my car trunk?" "Where are you when I have a pallet of mulch and every bag is ripped?"

I am a classic case of arrested development, having earned my undergraduate degree at age 36; my master's at 42, and began work on a Doctor of Education at age 66. I discovered that, much as universities like to tout their services to the "non-traditional" enrollee, they really don't know what to do with us old-as-hell students. I expected to be an anomaly in the doctoral program, but I didn't expect to be treated as a 35-year-old professional. When asked what my career goals were upon completion of the program, I answered honestly, "To be alive." At 115 lbs. I still felt like the elephant in the room (even though we met mostly online). Advisers and faculty never acknowledged my age, which would have been refreshing. I mean, isn't it obvious that someone who earns their doctorate at age 72 would have different aspirations than a fresh-faced young Ed.D. ready to take on the world?

Another assumption about us oldsters of both sexes is that we continually struggle with technology. OK, while I just had to call my 8-year-old granddaughter to find out how to change the background on my iPhone, I'm pretty good at keeping up with the latest apps, social media and who's who on YouTube. Go ahead, just ask me what prank the Merrell Twins are playing on their endless parade of boyfriends this week, or what Savannah LeBrant is wearing while she swims tirelessly around in that pool with her drop-dead-gorgeous husband the their devastatingly cute little girls. What I can't answer is how these YouTube stars make more money than you and I could ever dream of… and why we didn't think of it first!

So forgive my rant on being patronized. Why is it, that after we turn 65 (or 60 in many cases), people feel they must call us pet names, talk to us in LOUD simple sentences, and compare us with vegetables? A few years ago, NPR conducted a poll, asking older adults what terms they preferred to describe their age group. Senior citizens? Definitely not. Seniors? Close, but no cigar. Older adults? Preferred, but not perfect. An organization in the UK submitted "Super Adults" which the pollsters liked.

Because it conjures up an image of an old person in a cape and tights, I'm not crazy about being called a "Super Adult." Hey, here's a novel idea! Why not refer to us as individuals and not as a pack of wrinkled human beings, joined at the hip with similar characteristics and interests. My name's Barb. What's yours?

Why Do Old People Know This Stuff?

Ask a millennial to calculate a percentage and you get, "deer in the headlights!"

Abigail Trafford of the Washington Post may have referred to us as the generation of "dentures, decline and dysfunction," but we possess superior knowledge that will disappear when we no longer walk this earth. I've spent the past week jotting down some things that over-65s can do with our eyes closed. (That's good, since a lot of us close our eyes whenever we sit down!)

You can talk all you want about modern educational theory, but there was something to be said about the old "drill and kill" technique employed by most teachers (and ALL nuns) in the 1950s and 60s. It left certain facts burned into our brains. Sixty years later, we still know …

Units of Measure – Go ahead, ask me how many feet in a rod, or even if there's such a thing as a rod. Forced to memorize the endless tables in the back of our arithmetic books, my fellow 1969 high school graduates and I can recite ounces in a gallon, cups in a quart, feet in a mile and pounds in a ton. Amazingly, we can do this from memory without consulting Google, Wikipedia or Siri. This is my dirty little secret, but at Mother of Mercy High School I won the coveted title of Betty Crocker Homemaker of the Year, simply because I knew the difference between "tsp." and "Tbsp." and that "c." is an abbreviation for "cup" and not "cuspidor." The fact that a woman, who at age 25 had to call her mother to find out how to get fruit into Jell-O, could wear the Betty Crocker sash, is testament to the power of enforced memorization.

Percentages – Both of my children excelled in math. They aced the college-prep curriculum of algebra, geometry and trig and reached a high percentile on the math section of the ACTs. Ask them what 30-percent of $30 is and they still grab the old iPhone. Boomers can glide through

Wal-Mart without any tech support and come out reasonably close on their total cost of groceries. It's like I told my granddaughter, "You just KNOW." Multiply fractions? A cinch. Long division? Bring it! Are you allowed to move a decimal point? You betcha'! There is something comforting knowing how to solve a math problem, even when you don't have to. "Hey Alexa, the answer is 23. Now ask me another one!"

Diagramming Sentences – Every afternoon in the 7th grade, Sr. Conrad would lock our classroom door, break out the waterboard and spend two hours diagramming sentences. There were straight lines, slanted lines, lines for prepositional phrases, nouns in apposition, and clauses that were not related to Santa. We all became victims of Stockholm Syndrome; held captive but clinging to our captor as we learned to break apart the English language until there was no joy left in reading. Today, even while enjoying a work of light fiction, I automatically begin constructing little fortresses to house each sentence and divide it into unlikeable pieces. Someday, when I'm a contestant on Jeopardy, Alex Trebek will give me my choice of categories. "I'll take Hell is Like a Diagram for $1,000, Alex."

Cursive – So…the hours that we didn't spend diagramming sentences, we spent perfecting our penmanship. Cursive was obscenely important to 1950s elementary school nuns. They must have read the same study, concluding that those who make "lazy r's" would distance themselves from the Catholic church and wind up pole dancing with the Presbyterians. Not on my watch, dear! As a lefty, I was doomed from the start. With fountain pens being the only writing instrument permitted, I consistently dragged my pinky finger across the freshly applied ink. My cursive was one giant smear. Take me to your nearest pole.

Roman Numerals – Truly a lost art, especially when called upon to create an outline carved into stone with a chisel and hammer. I actually remember cramming for a Roman numeral test! There was some value in being familiar with this archaic art form, however. "Lives of the Saints," a must-have book to read during Mass, was paginated in Roman numerals. This made it very easy to look up famous martyr torture pictures, which were then passed around to elicit shock and awe from pew-mates. My favorite was the depiction of St. Sebastian, looking like a Botticelli angel while nine arrows protruded from his body. He was the ultimate trooper, a smile forever on his lips as he adorned page XLIII.

There are a few other skills that us old folks have perfected that I cannot attribute to the teaching prowess of our nuns and "lay" teachers. Most of us can still drive a stick shift (although double-clutching gets difficult with arthritis). We can write a check and blow a giant bubble with one piece of Bazooka. As the pandemic has us relying more on survival skills, like baking our own bread and chalk painting furniture, the lost arts of the 50s and 60s will serve us well. Why, just the other day, I needed a place to store all of my prepositional phrases and a total stranger asked if I knew how St. Polycarp met his demise.

In the Name of Shopping

"Marema" Takes on Coronavirus

Marema. Her name was a mash up of "Mary" and "grandma," and she wore it like a royal birthright. Starting with her grandchildren, the popularity of the name swept through the western suburbs of Cincinnati until everyone forgot Mary Jane Lockard and knew her simply as "Marema." And Marema wouldn't have liked this pandemic stuff!

She lived to be 93, no small feat in a family where the average lifespan is about 65. In her waning years, she lived with my sister and became increasingly more skeptical as time passed by. She got her knowledge of medicine from watching episodes of "Sex Sent me to the ER," and her legal acumen from "Judge Judy." With these as reference points, she was quick to de-bunk any news that came across her big-screen TV.

Marema (my mother) passed away on Memorial Day, 2016. It's probably best that she left us before coronavirus came to visit. Always one for black humor, I can't help but imagine what kind of conversation would have ensued when news of the virus broke.

Marema: "So, what do you think about this pandemic thing? I think it's a bunch of bunk."

Me: "Well, Mom, it's a pretty serious thing and we should all respect our governor's wishes to shelter in place."

Marema: "I never heard anything so ridiculous. They're making us all stay home, and I don't even know of anyone who has it."

Me: "That's because everyone you know has been voluntarily sheltering at home since 1996."

Marema: "I'm going out. I'll just go down to Meijer's. Nobody there is contagious."

Aha, now we'd be getting to the meat of the matter! Her concern for her own and the nation's health would be overshadowed by the curtailing of her daily trip to Meijer.

You see, Marema was a shopper; a consumer of the weird and grotesque. One Christmas, we all received alarm clocks shaped like chickens, resembling some group voodoo sacrifice. She loved markdowns. "Got these clocks for $1.50. They were originally marked $19.95!" There was nothing more satisfying for her than getting 70% off the ticket price. The fact that we did not want or need the objects purchased made little difference. It was the thrill of the chase.

Her Meijer trips were half-day excursions. Located just a few miles from her house, the big box emporium required some tricky maneuvering to arrive safely in the parking lot. I say "tricky," because Marema did NOT make left turns. The woman, who got her license in 1938, had managed to elude all left turns during her long driving career. 'Hey, Mom," I'd say while a passenger. "Why are we driving 20 miles to go to a restaurant that's three miles away?"

"Well, we don't want to <u>have</u> to make a left turn," she'd reply exasperated.

In her 80s and 90s, her vehicle of choice was a 1999 Geo Prizm. She had traded in a K-car, whose key had become firmly stuck in the ignition. Marema decided to remedy this by throwing a brown, fuzzy blanket over the steering wheel, covering the errant key. This was in case "someone" would want to steal her primer-covered Plymouth Reliant. A true masochist, no doubt.

Meijer not only satisfied her strong shopping urges but was also her social life. Her routine was always the same. Pull up and wait for an employee to bring her an electric riding cart. On the rare day that all the carts were in use, her reaction was akin to hearing that a tornado had devastated Bridgetown, or Graeter's was out of bittersweet syrup. In her phone call that evening, she'd sigh and say, "Well, there were no carts today. What are all those damn people doing in those damn carts?"

When things did manage to go smoothly, she'd glide through the store, talking with Shirley in produce (you know she's had seven surgeries this year), and Bob in the meat department. Her hoarding instincts always sharp, she'd search the store for a sale on capri pants. Today's pandemic hoarders had nothing on her. A few months after mom's death, my sister counted 47 pairs of capri pants in her closet. We tried to find a charity that would take them, perhaps one that catered to older, fashion-conscious women, but to no avail. Remember that song, "Timothy," when the mine collapsed and the other miners allegedly ate Tim? The refrain was, "Where on earth did you go?" Well, I often wonder, where on earth did those capri pants go? My sister's not talking.

Even though it's been nearly four years since her death, I can conjure up an image of Marema defying the stay-at-home order, taking her cue from Mel Gibson in Road Warrior. She'd ride recklessly through Meijer in a fully-charged electric cart, perhaps with a few heads hanging from her Izod belt. Pandemic be damned! There were new markdowns and piles of capris to conquer!

There's a Difference Between "Karen" and Kvetching!

Complaining is Good for the Soul.

My husband's family uses a lot of Yiddish words. An all-time favorite is "kvetch," which, literally, means to complain or whine. A good "kvetcher," however, can raise common complaining to an art form. Some folks can kvetch all day, every day... not about any specific offense, but about the state of things in general. Kvetching is usually preceded by "Oy," as in "Oy, my grandchildren!" or "Oy, my arthritis!" Good kvetching can transcend any age or gender. It's something in the DNA.

Unless you're living under a rock, you've, no doubt, heard the lexicon, "Karen," used to refer to middle-aged women who take people to task for real or perceived insults against them or their kids, spouses, etc. Known as "talk to the manager Karen," she is described as a soccer mom with one of "those" haircuts who comes out swinging when she feels she's been wronged. Unfortunately, the name now has racist overtones and has taken on a negative political connotation. Oh Karen, what have you become?

Us old folks are safe. Most of us aren't "Karens," we're "Kvetchers." We're from an era when gas station attendants (Yes, there were attendants!) would clean your windshield and even check the air in your tires. This service was offered complimentary with the weekly purchase of "Two dollars regular." These days, we are driven beyond human endurance by carelessness, incompetence or cluelessness, but instead of going on the attack, we just marvel at what the world has become and... kvetch!

Case in point. Since the start of the "damn COVID" most of us have utilized curbside pick-up for groceries or meals. A few weeks ago, I navigated the Panera online ordering system to pick up a kids' mac and cheese and bowl of tomato soup. First, let me add that I have a minor in computer science and can operate my iPhone successfully most days. Ordering through the Panera app took at least 15 minutes. . . Select – kids' size, little people's size. . . add to order. . . subtract from order. . . edit order. . . choice of sides. . . baguette or stale baguette, ad infinitum, ad nauseum. Oh yes, you have to indicate the model and year car you'll be driving, the VIN number and submit a CARFAX report. Once the order is completed, you have a choice of when to pick up. . . immediately, in an hour, next Tuesday or Christmas 2023.

Indicating I would claim my order post haste, in a few minutes I was sliding into one of the two, reserved "curbside pick-up" spaces. Easy-peezy, I thought. There is even a little button on the app that says, "I'm here!" I hit the button and waited. Ten minutes later, I hit the button again . . . and again. "I'm here! I'm here! I'm here!" Nothing. Not wanting to don my PPE to go inside, I waited another 10 minutes before giving up. I walked, silently fuming, into the near empty Panera dining room and was greeted by a friendly cashier.

"I was supposed to get a curbside pickup order," I said.

"Really, Ha-Ha, Sorry!" she chirped. "It's right there on the curbside pickup shelf."

I grabbed my now cold order and headed for the door. Did I yell? No. Did I ask to talk to the manager? No! Did I spend the rest of the day kvetching? You're damn right I did. "Oy, those restaurants!"

Even our highly trained physicians aren't exempt from the kvetch. Last year, I waited several weeks for an appointment with a well-known heart surgeon. He sent me for tests and that's the last I heard. Like a true kvetcher, I figured the news was just too grim to call me with the results. After another week, I called his office and got "Megan."

"Hi Megan," I said. "I've been waiting for some test results and haven't heard anything so thought I'd call."

"Really! Ha-Ha! Sorry!" Megan laughed as though I just recited a dirty limerick.

"We moved and this place is just a mess," she chortled. (Let me tell you, it doesn't inspire confidence when your heart surgeon's office is "just a mess.") I wanted to tell Megan that this wasn't a sinus headache we were talking about, but she offered to have the doctor call me . . . when she could locate him.

A few days later, I received a brusque call from the surgeon himself.

"Ha-Ha! Sorry!" he began the conversation. "Your test results were here all along buried on my desk. This place is just a mess."

I hung up and decided to take my chances with WebMD and the Wikipedia listing for "heart surgeries." It's more than a year later and I'm still alive, so it was probably the right choice! Bet that "Karen" doesn't have heart problems.

This summer, I visited another specialist and, again, tests were ordered. The very next day I received results through a highly sophisticated online application known as "MyChart." Well It may have been "my chart," but the results made no sense to me. The following week, I received a call from (she's baaack) Megan.

"Hello, this is Megan with your test results. The doctor said to tell you they are normal."

"Hey, did you used to me at the heart surgeon's office," I quizzed Megan.

"Yes, that place was such a mess. Now I'm here," she said proudly.

"Well, Megan, the results are well out of the normal range. How do you explain that?"

Megan paused for a minute and answered, "That's what the doctor told me to tell you."

Two weeks later I received another call from Megan.

"Hello, Mrs. Lockard," she began, "This is Megan with your test results. You have the permissive gene, Munchausen's Syndrome by Proxy and triple-reversed DNA."

"What does that mean, Megan?" I asked. "I don't understand any of those terms."

"Well, that's what's written here. I just read it. I don't know what it means."

If you were a physician and had some complicated test results to communicate to a patient, wouldn't you do it, or assign it to another medical professional? I went back to WebMD to try and decipher the language. It's been more than a month and I'm still alive, so probably another good choice. "Oy, doctors!"

But my favorite kvetch, the all-time Klassic Kvetch, occurred about 5 years ago when I tried to call the Better Business Bureau on a company that promised much more than it delivered. My initial call went to voicemail where I was asked to leave my name and number. When no return call happened, I tried again. In fact, I tried five or six more times with no human contact and no returned calls. About a month later, I received a call from a BBB representative, asking my complaint. "What is the name of the company you wish to report," he yawned.

"The Better Business Bureau," I snapped back.

"We're the Better Business Bureau," he laughed.

"I know. I'm reporting you for poor customer service and failure to respond to inquiries."

"So, you're reporting the Better Business Bureau to itself," he marveled.

"Yes," I added. "Would you like more details?"

Truly, kvetching at its finest!

So while we may not have the moxie and sharply angled haircut of "Karen," us old folks can still complain with the best of them. Rather than talking to the manager, we spend the day talking to ourselves. (Mumble, mumble) "Oy, the world's gone to hell!"

(This post is dedicated to my sister, Karen, the most uncomplaining, nicest person you will ever have the pleasure to meet. Maybe she should change her name to Megan?)

Memories of Hoarding and Gouging

Today's Hoarding has Nothing on 1977!

As I watch a young mom leave Dollar General with a shopping cart full of toilet paper and more rolls possibly taped to her body, I reflect on less kinder, gentler hoarders. In London, Ohio during the winter of '77, I experienced not only the stockpiling of essential supplies, but price gouging, intentional hit-and-runs and obscenities written on the window of the local bank. My story…

What bought me to London was my ex-husband's bruised ego. An intrepid, small-town newspaper editor, he had a run-in with his publisher about his right to expose the mayor in a parking ticket-fixing scheme. He quit his job and, since my job was at the same newspaper, we both found ourselves out of work. In October 1976 "ex" received an offer from the Madison Press in London, so we packed up our 1972 AMC Gremlin; our 1974 Matador (OMG, we were such car dorks!) and headed to the central part of the state.

Arriving on a sparkling fall day, London didn't seem so bad. I was unaware that hidden underneath those piles of colorful leaves, a brutal winter lurked; a winter that would shake your faith in human nature and produce fuel-line freeze up anxiety. Did I mention that this was also a time of very high unemployment? By luck I snared a job with a local real estate broker as a secretary/assistant. A portent of things to come, the person I replaced was crying hysterically at her desk when I arrived for an interview. Little wonder, it was the first position I'd held where I had to cash my paycheck at the realtor's bank and deposit said cash into my own account. Knowing there were insufficient funds to cover my payroll check, this seemed an effective way of catching it on the first bounce.

We survived the holidays by traveling back to our beloved Cincinnati. My boss elected to winter in Florida, leaving me to manage an office building and slew of rentals with about $300 in the business checking account. It wasn't fun. I hated London, but we were getting by. At age 27 with a small paycheck, I felt that getting by was doing pretty well. Then it happened, January 28, 1977. Temperatures dropped to 5 to 10 degrees below zero, heavy snow fell and winds blew it into drifts that blocked the one road that connected our town to the interstate. We were isolated from delivery trucks, visitors and honest mechanics…not just for days, but for weeks!

The bank was the first to succumb, sending home staff and locking its doors at noon the day of the storm. Since this was pre-online banking, residents had no way to access cash or conduct transactions. Thus began notes taped to the windows besmirching the bank manager. "F-you, Denny!" was a major theme. "I need $50. How the hell am I supposed to get it?" Needless to say, "Denny" was never able to repair the damage to his reputation.

The one local supermarket had its shelves stripped of the essentials in the span of a few hours. Almost a week later, the Ohio National Guard saw fit to drop frozen Burger King patties to us from helicopters. This actually created sort of a party atmosphere in London, with folks showing up to watch the maneuverings of the "whirly bird" lowering cases of mostly beef patties down to the populace below. There existed in all of Madison County, just one pair of winter gloves and two toboggan hats. They were the property of the local men's shop and marked up to $30/each. They remained after the blizzard, testament to the fact that, even at 10 below zero, a rural Ohio resident would only pay so much to keep from freezing.

Cars wouldn't start, or once started, wouldn't move. While in a parking space downtown, the front wheel on my Gremlin froze and locked. I walked to work for a week before our handyman Clyde figured out how to thaw the front tire. I gave him $20 for his trouble and felt truly liberated for the first time in several days.

There were blood-curdling reports of cars being run off the road by tow trucks, only to have the truck turn around and offer to drag the victim out of a ditch for a fee that bordered on usury. I don't recall any acts of kindness, sharing or brotherly love. Remember, this was the 1970s. It should have been more laid back and helpful than our brutal, technology-fueled crisis of today.

We packed up our trendy AMC vehicles later that spring and left London. With no savings and no job prospects, we accepted the use of a free apartment from some friends for a few months and hightailed it back to Cincinnati and civilization. Somehow the thought of those frozen burgers hurtling out of helicopters was enough to make us face the gloomy prospects of unemployment. It's taken 43 years to purge that image from my mind. It was recently replaced by the sight of grocery carts piled high with Charmin, Cottonelle, and off-brand toilet paper. Surely this will live as long in my memory.

Oh, to be in East Jesus!

"We are dedicated to providing a working model of an improbable improvised community at the edge of the world." – eastjesus.org

When most mid-westerners think of California, they see palm trees, surfers, "Daisy Dukes, bikinis on top," and Disneyland. Few are aware of an arid area near the Salton Sea (yes there IS a sea in the California desert!) known as East Jesus, just up the road from Slab City.

I visited East Jesus, near Niland, California, little more than a month ago. This was before social distancing and a critical shortage of paper products. The residents of East Jesus have always been socially-distanced, if not from each other than from the rest of California and the world.

To present a full picture of East Jesus, I have to backtrack and explain Slab City and, to some extent, Salvation Mountain. Occupied by a variety of artists, squatters, artist/squatters, Slab City was "erected" on concrete slabs from an abandoned WWII Marine Corps barracks of Camp Dunlap. Wikipedia describes it as "a miniature de facto enclave of anarchy." (The major tourist attraction in Niland is Salvation Mountain, erected of straw bales and spray foam. . . but that's its own blog post).

Although a short distance down a dirt road in the same Sonoran Desert, East Jesus is not Slab City. There is a large sign to this effect stating in shaky bold letters, "East Jesus is NOT Slab City." For one thing, "Jesus" is more organized and has become a respected folk-art encampment. It is a 501(c)3 and owns the 30 acres on which it exists. Lest it sound too establishment, East Jesus is also home to a 1988 Mercury covered in Barbie Doll torsos. There are scattered signs displaying the sentiments of a creator who credits every evil conspiracy to the dolphins. ("They invented evolution and converted to Christianity so they could make Santa not real.")

Every town needs a place of worship and East Jesus is no exception. Although there doesn't seem to be scheduled services, there exists The First Church of the Chocolate Martini. (Yes, the congregation sells bumper stickers). After being warned through a Google search that the townies could be rude, we found the locals to be warm and welcoming and proud of their time machine and a wooly mammoth built from old tires.

We met Santa, complete with a long, white beard, who summers at his studio in Laguna Beach. Another resident lights up a doobie and invites my husband to "the Burn" (Burning Man). In the government's eyes, East Jesus may be a tax-exempt organization, but its residents are off the grid… right now, far from the dystopian fears of COVID-19, a crashing economy and a very scary election season.

As an older, middle class white woman, it's weird that I find myself drawn to East Jesus and its inhabitants. Maybe I was always meant to be there? During these troubling times, the Jesus folks are probably spending their days creating art, attending services at the Chocolate Martini and obeying its credo, "Do Big Fun!" and "Make Good Thing!" Beats wasting away in Corona-ville.

The Pandemic and the Black (Lab) Plague

When Tybee Isn't Injuring or Damaging, He's a Pretty Nice Dog.

A few years ago I watched a program on Animal Planet about a couple who welcomed a pet bison into their home. The living room in the two-bedroom bungalow was dwarfed when this beast waltzed in to spend time with his "family." The huge eyes on the sides of his head seemed to take in his surroundings with the assurance that he could wipe out the flat screen and sectional with one well-aimed kick.

I couldn't understand how an otherwise normal man and wife could open their home to a 1,200-pound, smelly, clumsy animal. That is, until I met Tybee.

"Blanchard's Blue Hips-Don't-Lie Tybee" is our 7-year-old Black Lab. He's an American Lab, which means, like all things American, he's super-sized. Tybee recently weighed in at 100 lbs. even. His head is the size of a $12 Halloween pumpkin. I actually paid good money for him back in 2013 at age 12-weeks and already 32 pounds. I won't regale you with his puppy antics. Someday I'll write a book, but stand warned that it won't be another "Marley and Me." It will be more like "There's a Bison in My Nissan".

Tybee's (or our) misfortunes in the past month will more than make a hefty blog post, thank you! The most memorable incident occurred on a Saturday night in late July. I had fallen asleep watching Schitt's Creek when I was awakened by the sound of my husband yelling from the family room. I ran in to find him bleeding profusely from his nose and mumbling something about the "damn dog."

"Oh no, did he jump up on you?" I asked.

"No. . . he's loose . . . think I broke my nose!"

Like most obedience school drop-outs, Tybee doesn't understand commands like, "heel," and "stay." My husband had taken him out, and somewhere in the dark, Tybee saw movement. Now, this is a dog that has a cement block for a toy and who once tore the deck off the back of our house. When he wants to check something out, he simply lunges in that direction. Luckily, I'm too weak to hold onto him, but my brawny husband tried to hang on. . . dumb. He fell, nose down on to our drought-hardened lawn and proceeded to be dragged about 10 feet. Not a pretty picture.

As we tried to stem the flow of blood, Tybee galumphed around the front yard, daring me to catch him in between ice packs, tourniquets and searching for a sling. (Jerry had landed on his elbow before his nose hit the earth). It probably took my husband a week to recover, while Tybee was back in rare form the next day, taking up residence on our coffee table. . . on his back with all four legs in the air. I know what a friend of ours meant when she said that living with Tybee was like living with John Belushi's character in Animal House.

Silly me! I had thought I could remedy Tybee tearing himself from our hands by purchasing a "Wacky Walker." This is a leash made of something like a heavy-duty hose that stretches when pulled, then snaps back. The theory is that when a dog lunges, the leash has just enough "give" to keep it from being torn from your grip. It's nice in theory, but unless you're a WWF star, your chances of holding onto a monster rubber band with a 100-lb. bullet on one end are pretty much nil.

A Lesson Not Learned

Two weeks ago, while walking Tybee in broad daylight, something caught his eye. I immediately recognized the stiffening of his body; the pricked-up ears and that moment of perfect stillness before the lunge. Had I been better prepared, I might have stopped him from running across the road and tearing after. . .what was it? Then I saw the flash of a white tail and began praying. "Please God, let the skunk outrun Tybee." But ours is a vengeful god, and the skunk caught Tybee square in the face.

With that, Ty proceeded to run back to me, smearing me with skunk scent in the process.

We returned from our walk, both pariahs in our own home. Jerry forbade us entrance, so Tybee was relegated to the backyard and I was thrown a change of clothes and a bowl of hydrogen peroxide, Dawn detergent and baking soda. After bathing in the concoction twice, I was admitted to my house. My canine companion had fared much worse and was insanely rubbing his eyes and nose into the dirt to stop the burning.

Since SOMEONE had to wash "the dog," I suited up in muck boots, a Goodwill winter jacket, garden gloves and swim goggles. Using the magic mixture, I dumped it on Tybee, making sure to douse his big, pumpkin head. Two baths and he was tolerable. Some dry shampoo and commercial skunk smell remover and we allowed him in the house. It's amazing. Two weeks out and there is still a faint odor of skunk. A costly venture, I also had to replace a pair of running shoes, collar and leash, not to mention purchasing skunk odor remover and Skunk B-gone Room Freshener.

I fantasize that someday Tybee will valiantly save us from our burning house. As we hang onto his collar and let him lead us to safety, I'll get blessed revenge on friends and relatives who wonder why we put up with and, yes, even love him. Reviewing his history of eating all of the Christmas baking in 2016; destroying a $900 pair of trifocals; shredding a box of my City Council campaign materials; eating 200 probiotics and tearing all the phone and cable wires off the house, I think a bison might be easier. They don't chase skunks. . . but probably wouldn't save you from a burning building.

Backyard Pools, Whirly-Thingys and Bullfinches

Like the coronavirus, they grow exponentially. They won't stop until they've beaten us!

It started innocently enough. I had heard the rumor back in March that community pools and swim clubs would not be able to open this summer. Whatever would my poor grandchildren do? Sad enough they had been cheated out of timed math tests, arguing on the playground and biting friends at daycare. We could not let them suffer a lack of aquatic enjoyment when the temperatures climbed.

I suggested to my daughter that she might look into purchasing an above-ground, backyard pool . . . and gave it no more thought. Although it wasn't Wuhan, China, nonetheless, a new virus was spawned. Not realizing that backyard pools are considered declasse, I listened to my daughter's explanation of why she couldn't have a pool on her own property, but MY yard would be the perfect location. (In many circles, I am already considered trashy and low class, so it wouldn't make any difference)!

With no cure or effective preventive measures, the "tan-demic" took hold in our county. Hundreds of households succumbed to parental guilt, grabbing up Easy-Sets until they were scarcer than Lysol Disinfecting Wipes. As temperatures soared briefly in late May, we all decided to set up our pools at virtually the same time. But it was going to be easy, right? After all, the name is <u>Easy</u>-Set. According to directions, you just throw it on the ground, fill it with water and, voila…you're in an Esther Williams movie!

No Easy Button Here

My daughter and son-in-law showed up late on a Saturday afternoon, planning an hour or two to get the pool ready. Oh yes, they brought a level and their high school geometry books to figure angles, cosines, etc. "Not level enough," said my son-in-law quietly and disappeared in his truck, returning with a Rototiller. "If this doesn't do it, I'm coming back with an excavator." Easy-Set. E-a-s-y SET!

After a few hours of Rototilling, cleaning mud off of endless shoes and obsessive measuring, they put down tarps and spread out a flacid, Easy-Set pool. Seems like the "ring" that's the key to the entire pool structure, needed inflating. Home goes my son-in-law, back he comes with an air compressor. The ring is inflated and it's time for the hose. My husband, who has been observing this from behind his Leinenkugel's Summer Shandy, is put in charge of the filter. (No doubt for the same reasons that I am put in charge of the napkins and Cool Whip on Thanksgiving.)

By 10 p.m. the pool is almost full, kids are excited and tired and we are out of Summer Shandy. Softly, silently, the second invasion begins. A lone maple tree whirly-thingy spins down from the heavens and lands in the pool. At 10:01 p.m., 3,000 maple tree whirly-thingys land on the pool's surface and we scramble to put on our cheap Big Lots cover. Whew! We'll need to buy a skimmer tomorrow.

On Sunday at noon, the thermometer says 90-degrees and the grandkids show up to christen the pool. The 8-year old helps skim and I tell her I'll pay her a penny for each maple tree whirly-thingy she brings up from the bottom. The 2-year-old is dressed like he's going swimming in plutonium. Swim trunks, check. Rashguard shirt, check. Sunproof hat, check. SPF 160, check. $29.95 floating dragon with leg holes, check. He climbs up the ladder and climbs back down. He's fascinated by the ladder and screams when you try to put him in the water. The 8-year-old is now on a float with a Diet Coke and bag of Baked Lay's, two contraband treats from grandma's kitchen.

A Battle Lost/A Battle Won?

Those who know me, know that I am NOT a clean-freak, perfectionist or maple tree whirly-thingy obsessive. Still, there is something about THAT pool. I began venturing out before bedtime, just to skim off a few more "thingys" before retiring for the night. I breathed a sigh of relief when the cover was in place, protecting my $63 worth of chemicals, now dissolved in the 15-foot in diameter, 42" deep pleasure pit. But peace was short-lived. I came to the frightening realization that for as many maple tree whirly-thingys you skimmed off, more would take their place. I did research.

Did you know that the true name for maple tree whirly-thingys is "samara"? (Samara/corona? Very similar.). One tree can produce more than 100,000 whirlys and some can lie dormant in the ground for years, only to grow into another maple tree that produces…you guessed it! The samaras are also a favorite delicacy of the Bullfinch, so now a third invasion, masses of Bullfinches, looms on the horizon. It's all part of a grand conspiracy.

As the days passed, the more debris that fell into the pool, the more determined I became to keep it clean. I had the pH checked. More chemicals. I bought a small pool vacuum and when I discovered it wouldn't affix to the handle, took to holding my granddaughter by her feet while she dragged the vacuum across the pool floor. ("C'mon Caroline. Shelley Winters held her breath for 6 minutes in *Poseidon Adventure*. You should be able to do 90 seconds!")

Then, about a week ago, our pool…MY pool, experienced its first Northwest Ohio thunderstorm. Caroline had just finished gasping for air after a bout of vacuuming, when the wind picked up and unleashed a whirly-thingy maelstrom. I commandeered her to help drag the cover over the top of the pool, but the drawstring snapped and it was all I could do to keep the cover from blowing into one of the "nice" neighborhoods. "Caroline," I screamed. "Go get something to hold this cover on!" It was pathetic, watching her run toward the house on skinny, muddy legs. Five minutes later, she returned with a Coldren Crates Funeral Home chip clip and a hair scrunchy. The cover wouldn't hold, the pool filled with seeds and sticks, and I was beaten...a beaten woman. They found me, stretched out in a recliner chair watching YouTube and mumbling about alkalinity and automatic skimmers.

Just yesterday, chaos became order. The maple tree whirly-thingys were, miraculously, gone. Storms had cleared, chemicals were balanced and I sat victoriously on our deck congratulating myself for surviving the onslaught of attacks on my pool. All was right with the world. As I stared heavenward to give thanks, I saw a small wisp of fluff free itself from our giant cottonwood tree. Softly, silently, it fell onto the pool's surface.

Five Things I'd Like to See in the Internet of Things

Why Hasn't Some I.T. Genius Thought of This?

It's not just the Internet anymore. It's the "Internet of things." Simply put, it's all that stuff we have that's connected to the World Wide Web. Used to be you needed something the size of the Cray Supercomputer to access the global knowledge base. Now, our coffeemakers, hairdryers and Happy Meal toys are all happily connected in the online community and streamlining our lives…supposedly.

If COVD-19 has shown us anything, it' the value of being able to sit in our jammies while performing our jobs and making social contacts. We can chat with colleagues on Zoom, display our meager talents on Facebook Live and order takeout without changing from our flannels into more public attire. In the few weeks of social distancing, however, I've discovered that the Internet of things is somewhat lacking in what it provides to many of us who are sheltering in place. I've jotted down a few suggestions for anyone skilled enough to turn them into actual applications (or whatever you call them):

 How about recipes with ingredients that you actually HAVE in your kitchen? There are a plethora of wholesome, family-friendly dishes like Cozy Lasagna Bake and Beef with Vegetables Au Poivre, but what about using up the supplies you've been stocking for times like these? Yep, give me a simple recipe using a half-bottle of Two-Buck Chuck from Trader Joe's, an expired Snack Pak pudding, a gallon jar of pickles with one pickle and lots of "juice," and an old sticky container of maple syrup. It could be like a challenging episode of Chopped, only without Ted Allen.

Teachers have done an outstanding job of converting in-classroom learning to an online format with extremely short notice. Our kids now have access to curriculum, complete with built-in rewards and hourly reinforcement. What they don't have is access to "drill and kill "delivered through the Virtual Nun. Think of it – a habit-clad avatar making your online student repeat multiplication tables ad infinitum, ad nauseum. Virtual Sister could give digital holy cards to those who memorized all the units of measure and spit them back without error. Guaranteed that these facts will stick in their minds forever, whether they want them to be there or not.

For overworked parents who find themselves de-ciphering a third-grade syllabus while attempting to explain organic chemistry to a high school junior – it's a "One Up" auto-comment generated by Facebook artificial intelligence! For those posts that exude self-satisfaction with the way that "Kendra is adapting splendidly to homeschooling," or "Xander just can't get enough of the German philosophers," your Facebook account will post a comment that's just slightly more impressive. Think of wowing your friends with, "Yes, it's all I can do to get Allison to quit trying to improve her math time tests," and "We know where Xander's coming from. Our 18-month-old just keeps saying, 'More Nietzsche, mama!' "Best part is that you don't have to feel bad about bragging…it's AI, right?

Doing a lot of network TV viewing lately, I've discovered a need for a new algorithm. Cottonelle is airing a 30-second spot that proclaims, "There will be toilet paper!" The company then boasts that it has partnered with United Way to serve those who need it most. My question? Where is the formula that determines WHO needs toilet paper the most? What factors are taken into consideration? Age? Size? Diet? Are there folks who have actually applied for a toilet paper stimulus package? Difficult to think about, but a quick online TP calculator would be beneficial during these times. (If I were a conspiracy theorist, I'd blame COVD-19 on those damn, singing Charmin bears!)

During this time of self-isolation and social distancing, I have vowed that I will learn a new skill. There are a lot of online learning resources for photography, music, languages, crafts and cooking. So, c'mon Coursera!

How about a quick class in gene-editing using CRISPR-DNA? You could download the app and mess around with your family's genetic makeup. This seems far more stimulating than learning how to make the perfect pie crust or carrying on a simple conversation in French. Besides, I've always wanted to know what it felt like to be a sheep!

Products of the Past Should STAY in the Past . . . or Should They?

Give Me a Good Dose of Geritol Delivered by Bishop Sheen!

Sometimes life resembles a Microsoft application. There are often just too many options. Growing up with three television channels was easier; boring, perhaps, but choosing among The Lone Ranger, Sky King and Tarzan was infinitely simpler than browsing 60 cable channels, hundreds of Netflix movies, and endless streaming services. Be careful what you ask for.

In the 1950s and 60s, there were so few products of a particular ilk that those products became household words. Some of them were said to be endowed with magical powers, when, in truth, they weren't much more than a tarted-up vitamin or discarded pieces of factory-farm animals.

Created in August 1950, Geritol was touted continually on television as a product that could cure "iron poor, tired blood." Have to tell you that the word "tired" got my mother's attention, (boosted by the delivery style of Ralph Bellamy, Geritol spokesperson.) My mother was always tired. It occurs to me that lots of women were tired in the 50s... tired of being stuck at home, tired of cooking, cleaning and watching "Queen for a Day" on TV (more about that later). Mom liked Geritol and said the "tonic" made her feel more energetic. Could it be that the 12 percent alcohol content had something to do with that euphoric feeling?

Later, Geritol became the brand name for several vitamin supplement products. After an FTC investigation, the product had to limit its healing description to "helping those with iron deficiency anemia." Geritol is still with us and has gained some respectability as a supplement; however, some recent online customer reviews attribute its powers to increasing dreams, boosting your chances of getting pregnant, and curing knee pain. On one Geritol Q&A site, a customer asked if llamas could take Geritol.

It was at this point that I discontinued my sketchy research into Geritol's benefits.

Another one of Mom's favorites was Knox Unflavored Gelatin. Now, there are few things that taste worse than unflavored gelatin. First, gelatin is the by-product of animal bones, skin and connective tissue. Now, think about mixing that sugarless, flavorless substance in warm water and drinking it every day. Mom's "gelatin time" was 3 p.m. and I can remember her grimacing as she forced down a cup of the colorless liquid. The Knox box had a sketch of a cow on the front, a testament to its bovine origins. Oh yes, Mom subjected herself to this ritual for years for the sole purpose of strengthening her fingernails. It was just something that you did, like eating carrots for your eyesight and bread crusts for curly hair. Being a vegetarian and someone who's not into gagging, I've never tried the gelatin cure. It's spared me a lot of anguish, but I have to admit, I do have pretty crappy nails.

In the gelatin realm, there was also the all-purpose lemon Jell-O. If you weren't sure what to do with a food-type substance in the 50s and 60s, you put it in lemon Jell-O. One of the worst recipes I ever came across was Veg-All, a canned concoction of random, tasteless vegetables, suspended in a pie plate of lemon Jell-O. Mom shaved carrots and celery into the bouncy, lemon, animal by-product in an effort to trick us into eating our veggies. I once had dinner at a friend's house where the dessert was blueberries in lemon Jell-O. The family called it "floating eyeball salad." A 50s housewife could feed her brood for a week with just lemon Jell-O, Miracle Whip, Heinz Ketchup, Velveeta and Creamettes on the shelf. Throw in some cans of tuna and you could eat for a month.

Like health supplements and food products, there were entertainment venues that were memorable, simply because they were among the few offerings available in the age of Sputnik and the Cold War. Bishop Fulton J. Sheen, known as the country's first televangelist, rivaled Milton Berle and Frank Sinatra in the ratings with his hour-long show, "Life is Worth Living." The format was simple. The Bishop would talk in front of a live audience, no script and no cue cards. Occasionally, he'd use a blackboard to drive home a theological point. "Life" ran from 1950-57, followed by "The Fulton Sheen Program," 1961-68. Bishop Sheen stuck with a winner and used the same, talking-head, unrehearsed format that earned him two Emmy Awards.

My husband, who is Jewish, used to roller skate in his basement to Bishop Sheen and also the weekly radio broadcast of the rosary. To illustrate our different approaches to life, know that my Catholic friends and I skated to Jan & Dean and later on to Michael Jackson's "Off the Wall," while Jerry perfected his salchow to the cutting-edge sound of Bishop Sheen. He has turned out far more sensible than I.

Perhaps the worst (or best) show on 50s television, depending on your point of view, was "Queen for a Day." Misogynistic, voyeuristic, and preying on the misfortune of others, "Queen for a Day," featured the heartfelt stories of women ranging from needing a washing machine to do laundry for 12 kids, to acquiring medical equipment to keep herself and "the twins" alive.

Jack Baily, Queen's gifted host and interviewer, pulled such emotional stories from the guests, that they had my mother crying every day at 2 p.m. while she ironed my dad's handkerchiefs. The show was broadcast from the "beautiful Moulin Rouge" hotel with a live audience shown sitting at tables and eagerly waiting for the next sob sister. The daily winner was determined by an applause meter (really!) and donned a red cape and crown while she paraded down a runway (at the beautiful Moulin Rouge). Oh yes, the day's Queen received some high fashion items of clothing along with her major ask. We all know that Chanel is something every woman wants, right after food and medical care for her children!

What happens in Vegas stays in Vegas, and some things from the past need to STAY in the past. Surely, our choices of food, entertainment and health products have grown exponentially in the past six or seven decades. Unfortunately, what constitutes a prize-winning sad story has become much sadder in this era of COVID-19, racial strife and political name-calling. Still, would it be all bad to have a handy cure-all like Geritol tonic, a quick meal staple like lemon Jell-O and Bishop Sheen's inspirational words on a daily basis? I fear we would laugh at their simplicity now in 2020. Not sure about you, but simplicity might be just what the doctor ordered.